C000217453

Coaching Behind Bars

Coaching in Practice series

The aim of this series is to help coaching professionals gain a broader understanding of the challenges and issues they face in coaching, enabling them to make the leap from being a 'good-enough' coach to an outstanding one. This series is an essential aid for both the novice coach eager to learn how to grow a coaching practice, and the more experienced coach looking for new knowledge and strategies. Combining theory with practice, the series provides a comprehensive guide to becoming successful in this rapidly expanding profession.

Published and forthcoming titles:

Bluckert: *Psychological Dimensions to Executive Coaching*
Brockbank and McGill: *Coaching with Empathy*
Brown and Brown: *Neuropsychology for Coaches: Understanding the Basics*
Driver: *Coaching Positively*
Hawkins: *Creating a Coaching Culture*
Hay: *Reflective Practice and Supervision for Coaches*
Hayes: *NLP Coaching*
Paice: *New Coach: Reflections from a Learning Journey*
Pemberton: *Resilience: A Practical Guide for Coaches*
Rogers: *Developing a Coaching Business*
Sandler: *Executive Coaching: A Psychodynamic Approach*
Vaughan Smith: *Therapist into Coach*
Wildflower: *The Hidden History of Coaching*

Coaching Behind Bars

Facing Challenges and Creating Hope in a Women's Prison

Clare McGregor

Mc
Graw
Hill
Education Open University Press

Open University Press
McGraw-Hill Education
McGraw-Hill House
Shoppenhangers Road
Maidenhead
Berkshire
England
SL6 2QL

email: enquiries@openup.co.uk
world wide web: www.openup.co.uk

and Two Penn Plaza, New York, NY 10121-2289, USA

First published 2015

Copyright © Clare McGregor, 2015

All rights reserved. Except for the quotation of short passages for the purposes
of criticism and review, no part of this publication may be reproduced, stored
in a retrieval system, or transmitted, in any form or by any means, electronic,
mechanical, photocopying, recording or otherwise, without the prior written
permission of the publisher or a licence from the Copyright Licensing Agency
Limited. Details of such licences (for reprographic reproduction) may be obtained
from the Copyright Licensing Agency Ltd of Saffron House, 6–10 Kirby Street,
London, EC1N 8TS.

A catalogue record of this book is available from the British Library

ISBN-13: 978-0-335-26442-1
ISBN-10: 0-335-26442-5
eISBN: 978-0-335-26443-8

Library of Congress Cataloging-in-Publication Data
CIP data applied for

Typeset by Aptara, Inc.

Fictitious names of companies, products, people, characters and/or data that may
be used herein (in case studies or in examples) are not intended to represent any
real individual, company, product or event.

Praise for this book

"A stark and thought provoking read, that totally makes sense! Having witnessed first-hand the importance of coaching, assisting and empowering a person who may have made a few ill-judged choices in life, to turn a bad situation good; I applaud the author for keeping it real, whilst demonstrating the true value of coaching."

James Timpson OBE, Chief Executive of Timpson

"During almost 40 years of working in all types of prisons I have not come across many people who were willing to volunteer their services to support prisoners, indeed until relatively recently this type of activity would not have been encouraged. I feel strongly enough about this initiative, having seen it in progress, to suggest that it has the potential to be as effective as any other intervention used in prisons to reduce re-offending.

This is a wonderful book, far more than a book about coaching, it provides a very accurate picture of life behind bars and allows the reader to view the prisoner as more than just an individual that society deems requires punishment, without really trying it shows that many of these women are victims themselves and require far more support than being locked up. That through this scheme 'we can unlock hope' is surely a wonderful testament that can restore our faith in human nature, this book certainly pulls at the heart strings and is also a must read for students of the Criminal Justice agencies."

Clive Chatterton, former Governor of Styal Women's Prison

"Focusing not on what offences have been committed but practical and tough solutions to help 'clients' achieve inner strength, Clare McGregor has changed the lives of women and staff at HMP Styal, largely with nothing more than a prisoner number, a bicycle and optimism. Claire is a star and the outcomes are stellar. To understand the reference, read the book – it will change your life and the lives of others – inside and out."

Felicity Gerry QC

"This powerful book took me back to my time in HMP Styal and made me question whether things would have been different if I had the opportunity to be coached by CIAO. I have literally 'laughed out loud' and cried at the insightful, emotive, yet oh so familiar content; which made me eagerly read

on. Major credit needs go to all the coaches and the women who have found themselves in Styal and taken the opportunity to be involved. Clare is one amazing woman who is real to herself and this shines through."
Natalie Atkinson, NUS Endsleigh Student of the Year 2014
and former prisoner in Styal

"Clare McGregor's book offers a wakeup call for those who see coaching as the preserve of only the rich and privileged. With raw, personal candour **Coaching Behind Bars** *describes Clare McGregor's reaction to the tough life of prison inmates. She also gives an insight into moments of joy and revelation. If you want to set yourself a challenging CPD task, this book sets the bar (the prison bars) very high indeed."*
David Megginson, Emeritus Professor of HRD, Sheffield Business School

"This is such a refreshing book. Amidst all the debate about what the nature of 'what works' and how financial mechanisms such as procurement and payment by results might improve rehabilitation this book provides an inspiring account of how people, when supported at the right time and in the right way turn their lives around. It is story about women in a women's prison and in that sense it's very particular. But it is also a universal story about human struggle, compassionate support and triumph against all the odds."
Clive Martin, CEO, Clinks

"This is a great book; it oozes humanity on every page. It is a challenging read - people not acquainted with the realities of crime and punishment will learn a lot about both from the powerful case studies and from the author's personal reflections. Those well acquainted with crime and punishment, through their work, will be challenged to rethink what they do and how they do it. Clare McGregor tells us that humans come up with better solutions by 'being curious [rather] than furious' (p6) but I think I disagree; it is the combination of both insatiable curiosity and consuming fury at human suffering and injustice that makes her and her book so special. As one woman she has coached puts it: 'you ask all the right questions'. Readers of this book should be prepared to be challenged (like anyone else Clare coaches) to come up with their own answers; but the author certainly helps us along the way."
Fergus McNeill, Professor of Criminology and Social Work,
University of Glasgow

"Prison is hardly ever about hope, choice or personal responsibility, and women's prisons in particular are suffused with a sense of loss, dependency and abject failure. Coaching Behind Bars offers prisoners the rare opportunity to begin to shape their lives and make plans for a life beyond custody and beyond despair."
Juliet Lyon CBE, Director, Prison Reform Trust

For those above and outside:

Jane, Mary and Newnham, you changed my life.

For those inside:

*This book is for everyone who has ever spent time in Styal
and, in particular, for the courageous women who choose
to change their future by working with those who make
Coaching Inside and Out such a joy:*

*Barbara, Belinda, Ben, Clare,
Evelyn, Gillian, Graham, Janice, Jan, Janet, Jeanne,
Judi, Jules, Jules, Liz, Liz, Mark, Mike, Rachel,
Shahida, Teresa, Vajramudita and Vanessa.*

Contents

Figures

Series Editor's Foreword

Most people's perception of coaching is that it is a high value service for highly paid executives or managers whose preoccupations are how to manage their tightly packed lives so that they get at least some leisure time, how to get yet more gloss into already glossy careers or how to manage their teams.

Imagine my surprise then when one day a while ago I read a blog by someone who was possibly crazy or just a naïve enthusiast. The blog was about coaching women in prison. What was this? Coaching for people who are among the most marginalized in our society, who are most probably very far from the 'resourceful' state we coaches like to go on about when we are taking care to distinguish ourselves from therapists? Yes, indeed. And furthermore this project was thriving. That was my introduction to Clare McGregor, not crazy at all, just an outstanding coach and a very hard woman to say no to, which is why her charity is now well established in many areas working with men and women in the community.

When you read this inspirational book you will find a lot of your preconceptions about prisons and prisoners challenged. Among Clare's many case studies there are women you will recognize as having similar problems to those senior executives with whom you normally work. You will get a unique view of what actually goes on in a prison and why there is no reason whatsoever why coaching should not work as well in a prison as it does anywhere else.

The book is also realistic about what coaching can and can't do. Just as in any other context, coaching sometimes works and sometimes doesn't and sometimes you don't know whether it has or not. It is a reminder of some of the core principles that we all learn during our training, for instance that coaching is not about that feeble concept, 'helping', though we all hope it is helpful, nor is it about advising, rescuing or reforming. Clients have to be volunteers – and they are.

This book celebrates the amazing resilience of the human spirit and shows that the discipline of coaching will work as well in a tough prison as it will outside. The criteria are the same: what do you want to change? What's holding you back? What assumptions are you making? What strengths do you have? How can you make a first step towards achieving what you want?

As the book says, 'Coaching Inside and Out has been able to realise that taking an approach that is all about self-determination, that is so valued and potent in industry, can still transform lives when it is taken into an environment that is perhaps the least self-determining you can get. If coaching can work there, it can work anywhere.'

Jenny Rogers
Series Editor

Acknowledgements

Stories in this book are unembellished. The lives and words of women in Styal do not require artistic licence. Elements from any case, however painful, are also rarely unique. That they could tell the story of many women adds to their weight. All Coaching Inside and Out's clients in this book gave permission for quotes and stories to be shared with the promise they would not be identifiable. If any information might identify someone they have agreed to that. Quotes were either captured by the coaches themselves or during the evaluation done by Graham Smyth of Manchester Metropolitan University. The quotes from staff are from a range of organizations and further care has been taken to ensure they are as unidentifiable as required.

Statistics are mostly taken from the Prison Reform Trust's essential information known as the *Bromley Briefings* (summer 2014 edition). Figures relate to England and Wales, unless otherwise stated, and can be found here along with the latest version: www.prisonreformtrust.org.uk/Publications/Factfile.

1 Getting stuck in

I stared at the heavy prison gate shivering uncertainly. It was a dank November day and I had no ID, no keys and no way out. My warm smile at the approaching officer vanished as I realized no one would ever let me through on my word alone. Then a passing woman shouted: 'Don't let her out, Miss! She's a prisoner!' This was when I began to wonder just how long my stay in Styal might be.

What on earth was I doing on the wrong side of a gate looking at a prison officer in sinking desperation? I do not mean: how had I not ensured I could get back out? I mean: why was I in Styal at all?

For the last 10 years my business had taken me into our prisons where many of society's and individuals' problems collide. I was asked to develop solutions and services to address problems such as mental health, prostitution and counter-terrorism. To strengthen this I also worked as an executive coach with charity chief executives, senior police officers and others.

During this time I relied on people to open and close prison gates for me. I had also been wise enough to stay close to someone with a bunch of keys chained firmly to a belt fastened tightly round their waist. However, that day I had been escorted to one building, walked to a meeting elsewhere, and left without realizing I had carelessly lost my identity and my freedom to come and go along the way.

Why was I here as a coach and not as a prisoner? I was 38 when I got stuck behind that gate. Little more than the average age in Styal of 34. Why had women done what they did to end up in prison over those years whereas I had not?

Do not think there are not 'women like me' or, indeed, people like you in prison. There are. Of course you can see stereotypes, if you look for them. Yet all of society is in there too. I have seen pale, ill-looking women come blinking into the sunshine from the depths of the wing, resembling prisoners in Siberian gulags. Others are like the best-dressed WAGs or your next door neighbour. I might easily be spending more time on the other side of the fence as a passionate person who has real problems with being ordered to do things. I do not always think everything through and speak my mind, often loudly. I do not understand many of society's unwritten rules and ignore a few of those I do. However, while regularly fallible in many different ways, like every one of us, this has never got me into trouble with the police.

When women are imprisoned it is not just about the crimes, it is about their life history too. The 'typical' woman in prison has been far less fortunate than most. Yet, even with all my family and friends behind me and problems coming just one at a time, I have occasionally found being human tough. Life is easily shaken to its core and our sanity is a fragile thing. Character in Styal is too often built in ways that scarcely bear thinking about. It is harder to make sense of right and wrong when your mother allowed your uncle into your childhood bedroom or your alcoholic father beat anyone within reach. Lack of security and self-esteem stemming from cruelty and poverty can also mean a woman feels unable to say no to a partner and commits crime as a result.

Accidents of birth explain a little of why I was not a prisoner. The motivation and energy to go in as a coach came from life's unfairness and was further influenced by the lives and deaths of people close to me. I know it is not as simple as this though. It is not just about nature and nurture. Luck plays its indefinable part. However, I have stayed out, so far, and am very grateful for that.

Moving to Alderley Edge was one of many chance events that enabled me to set up CIAO – the charity 'Coaching Inside and Out'. This village was rumoured to sell more champagne than anywhere else in Britain and to be entirely populated by Manchester's premier league footballers and *Coronation Street* stars. Alderley made eighth on a list of towns with the most millionaires. However, it does not totally live up to its reputation. My neighbour has a mangle to wring the water from her clothes, not a tumble drier.

We live within cycling distance of the only women's prison in the north-west, yet most drive straight past on their way to the airport without even realizing it's there. If anyone ever went into Styal, as a visitor or as a prisoner, I think they would want to change something; about themselves, their life or the society we live in. People ask if working in the prison is depressing and it really is not. It only feels powerless if you desperately want to help but do not have the time or resources. CIAO coaches can enable that change though: to play to our strengths, learn from our mistakes and help others to do the same.

This book is my personal experience of something all-absorbing, utterly exhausting and sometimes deeply painful. It is also the best thing I have ever done. I have responded to the turmoil of a woman's arrival at the prison in a 'sweat box', shared the challenges, frustrations, successes, failures and unexpected joys of progress, before seeing women standing alone at the roadside clutching their belongings in a bin liner once released.

This is my take on the challenges of coaching in a unique environment and its chapters reflect the charity's coaching model as well as illustrating our approach with tales of comedy and graphic pain. Our clients' own words give further insights into the reality of life behind bars: life without your partner, without your children and sometimes without hope.

Some might think prisoners unwilling or unresourceful and that coaching is only suitable for business high-flyers or those struggling at work. However, powerful professional relationships are still possible behind bars. Coaching should not just be for managers and people with money to spare. We have seen its impact on those many have written off completely and those who have given up on themselves. Everyone involved learnt far more about who we are and what on earth we are doing here than we ever expected. Coaching behind bars has changed my life as much as it has helped other people to change theirs.

The final chapter explains how CIAO's approach is spreading through our communities and prisons, including male offenders, veterans and those at risk of offending. CIAO has a simple aim: to challenge and support offenders to change their lives and the lives of others for the better using exactly the techniques we use successfully with leaders elsewhere. We show our clients that they are more than just a number and give them the tools to prevent them becoming one again. For me the real hope is how coaching can unlock the extraordinary potential in people within our criminal justice system.

It may yet go terrifyingly wrong for any one of us, though. I could still find myself on the wrong side of that gate for far longer. My husband has pointed out I could make a compelling case for time off in lieu for all the time I have spent inside already, if not for good behaviour.

2   Welcome to HMP & YOI Styal

When you arrive at a prison you generally have more questions than answers. When you set out to coach someone that is always the case. This chapter takes you through the prison gate as both a visitor and as a prisoner. It also explains what we mean by coaching and what led me to coach offenders without payment for nearly four years of my life. 'There is no better place to be in the north west right now than Cheshire East [with its] unique combination of great work opportunities, choice of house styles, friendly communities and breathtaking surroundings.' So says the latest council leaflet. Her Majesty's Prison and Young Offenders Institution Styal is in Cheshire East and is 'home' to 460 of our country's most damaged and damaging women, many of whose lives are challenging and chaotic. If you picture a prison, Styal is nothing like that. It is indeed in 'breathtaking' countryside, 12 miles from Manchester city centre and 2 miles from Manchester Airport. An officer described it as a village without a post office or a pub. The site was built as an orphanage in the 1890s under the Poor Law before morphing into a prison in the 1960s when women were moved in from Strangeways (now HMP Manchester).

A 'choice of house styles' include a modern wing but leafy avenues also separate Victorian red-brick houses, which each hold 20 or so women mostly in shared 'dorms'. Named after female reformers, authors and so on, these 'units' are referred to by the letter of the avenue they are on, using the International Phonetic Alphabet, and their numerical position from the main gate. An inspirational woman from history, such as Florence Nightingale, is thus abbreviated to B4 or Bravo Four. In 1999 the cells in purpose-built Waite wing more than doubled capacity. This broke with tradition by being named after locally born Terry, himself held hostage for years and who visits Styal regularly. Ugly portacabins squat between the buildings and a gentle slope downhill obscures highly secure units, the shed-like wing and workshops with 'work opportunities' at the far end.

Beehives near the high perimeter fence backing directly onto the afflu-ent commuter town of Wilmslow and the occasional passing pushchair or brood of ducklings add to the surreal atmosphere. This was the world into which I willingly and, to some extent, unwittingly stepped.

In contrast, many women come to Styal most unwillingly straight from court. About half do not expect to be imprisoned and many are in for the first time. Arrival impacts on more than just the prisoner her-self. Women have fears about children left with a neighbour or at home, parents or others they care for needing support, and pets going unfed. Women arrive in large white vans or escort vehicles referred to as 'sweat boxes'. These are huge on the outside and tiny on the inside. Once you step out of the van you are surrounded by high fences crowned with razor wire and can no longer walk through a gate without someone else unlocking it for you.

In 'Reception' you are given a prison number and photo ID card, as if it were your first day with a multi-national corporation. Your personal belongings are now known as 'property' and anything prohibited is taken until your release. You and your belongings are also searched for drugs or potential weapons. The human body's range of temporary storage areas means items can be smuggled inside in a most intimate fashion. As someone once said to me: 'If you can "pack" a ten pound baby you can "pack" a lot of drugs.' The days of full strip-searching are over for women, though, after concerns about dignity grew. Now only as much clothing and underwear is taken off as is necessary on grounds of risk and 'reasonable suspicion'.

As well as the many unfamiliar processes, you hear two alien lan-guages. I was virtually illiterate on starting but now speak semi-fluent 'prison' with conversational 'street'. As with any organization you need to understand and use the formal jargon with its numerous acronyms such as ROTL (rhyming with throttle). Plain English is left in a locker at the gate along with your ID. Elegant language is rare, even if you might guess 'pro-social' is the opposite of anti-social. 'Apps' are not useful telephone tools but the 'application forms' prisoners use to request most things. 'Association' is not a connection between two things but a set amount of 'free time' when prisoners are allowed out of their cells.

You must be able to interpret prison slang but there is no need for a coach to speak it, and I have baffled a few by doing so. Phrases can show the impact of life inside. While you might forget you are in a prison if you are a visitor, a client talked of half-fooling herself she was not really confined but admitted: 'I really saw the gates last week.' Language and cir-cumstance affect your mind both ways and I did wonder if I had worked in this field too long when I misheard someone say they worked in 'murders and acquisitions'.

What led us to coach prisoners for free?

At its simplest level this happened because I asked if I could do it and then asked if others would like to join me. At a deeper level this happened because my anger about the unfairness of the world developed into curiosity about how we might change it. Human beings come up with far better solutions through being curious than furious.

After eight years working with leaders and partnerships to reduce inequality, my work went quiet as the recession swallowed up public sector spending. Pausing for a day to draw breath it struck me that the professionals I coach are already brilliant but want to move up a level and do more to help others. Meanwhile, many people near rock bottom lack belief in their power to change anything at all. So it dawned on me that I could provide free coaching to those who might benefit most but are never normally offered it.

On 1 October 2010 I picked up the phone and rang the governor to ask if I could coach some women. Fortunately he had done a prison managers' coaching course himself and knew my work, so he wasn't under the illusion I meant kicking a football around. His immediate response was: 'When can you start?'

This was the start of a tailor-made challenge for me, particularly as a chief inspector of prisons had described Styal as: 'one of the most complex and demanding of institutions even amongst female prisons'. Or, as someone else put it: 'If you can do it in Styal you can do it anywhere.' I held onto this thought very tightly during the hard times ahead. My skills lie in bringing people together and helping individuals and organizations help others by developing themselves and their services. CIAO was a logical extension of this. Fortunately, running my own business as a social enterprise to benefit the community meant the money earned over the previous eight years paid for my time developing CIAO over the first four years of its life. I had also developed support networks that would be vital throughout that time.

My social enterprise is about the people society often turns its back on – the Others. Yet offenders are often victims themselves too, as our coaches have occasionally learnt in painful detail. Our start in life can set us back a long way, but does not necessarily mean we are doomed. Most pull through. Some cope and some manage to escape their circumstances through sheer luck and personality. A few are also dragged down later on in life. Our innate capacity for resilience, optimism and hard work is wrapped up in that.

There is a huge difference between standing in someone's shoes and being in their skin or locked in their mind. Would I have survived? Would I have chosen to carry on living? Justice is about so much more than being sentenced for a crime. Social and restorative justice can redress the balance by considering someone's entire life, seeing a different perspective and offering a real chance to change things. If we do this with those some might consider beyond hope then we can make life that little bit fairer and better for us all.

Crime and how we react to it should be everyone's concern. The majority of offenders have grown up in the same communities as their victims and the costs of their offending, both human and financial, are borne by those communities. Juries only vote to ostracize people temporarily nowadays: most offenders return to the place from which they were banished. I am also very aware that one difference between my professional and prison clients is that those inside have been caught and sentenced. This is not the same as saying those of us outside have never committed a crime.

Prison may appear to be the end of the line for the criminal justice system, but it is actually an opportunity for a new start. If you work from what some see as the bottom up then you are working where there is the most potential in our society: potential we cannot afford to waste.

Take my advice...I'm not using it

Few people are short of advice, CIAO's clients in particular. Coaching is far rarer, even from those who have our best interests at heart. A mentor can use coaching techniques to draw out someone's own solutions but can also share their own views or ideas. In contrast, CIAO holds the boundary that coaching offers very firmly. We do not signpost clients to other services. We do not tell them what to do. We are not there to rescue them. My first client put her finger on it when she asked: 'What would you do?' in our very first session. She laughed immediately as she realized that was a question I would never answer.

Mentoring is more practical and can involve activity – i.e. helping someone get to an appointment, whereas coaching is about encouraging thinking and self-direction – i.e. helping someone realize they will find a way to get to that appointment because the appointment will help them get what they want in life. A client said:

> I thought life-coaching would be: you'll be doing this, you'll be doing that, you'll need to do that. Now I know where I need to focus and that it has to come from me. That it can come from me.

For me the most useful and telling differentiator between coaching and mentoring is asking: 'Where does the wisdom and power lie in the relationship?' In mentoring, the wisdom lies with the mentor. In coaching, the power and wisdom lie with the client, not the coach.

What we are absolutely not doing is coaching in the sense of putting words into the mouth of a defendant or a witness. It is all about the client having their own voice. Coaches keep their own counsel: a really useful discipline for life. We do not pass on requests for action or information. Instead we can ask: 'Where can you find out? Who might know?' We encourage clients to look inwards for the answers and strengthen their skills rather than giving information. We help them realize they already have the capacity to make thoughtful decisions and the ability to find out more: 'You've made me realize I can do things. Just by making me think about it.'

People often ask what CIAO's model is. We look at the whole person and the reality of where they find themselves. We encourage and support them to think and take action for themselves, instead of telling people what we think they should do. Clients start by exploring how their life is today. The coach then takes their lead, looking at what they want to change and their ideas for making realistic goals a reality. We also look at the values that drive the client and assumptions that may be holding them back.

Developing a client's inner resources means they can find and make the most of external resources when coaching ends. 'It is empowering. It enables me to tap into my own resources and build on my strengths...to tap into my...values and build out from that.' This approach builds self-reliance and self-belief but also makes it much more challenging for clients. By focusing on their needs and strengths, clients really believe they can change things and start to do so. What we do is listen, watch, question, challenge and support. One-to-one discussions and opportunities to reflect with a trusted outsider help clients explore their strengths and limiting beliefs. Being challenged in a non-threatening way, with honest feedback about what we do and how we think, can change lives. It has certainly changed mine.

I love the freedom of mentoring but am in awe of what the discipline of coaching can achieve.

3   What are you doing here?

What attracts a coach to work in a prison and what attracts prisoners to work with a coach, when neither really has an idea what they are letting themselves in for until they sit down next to one another? This chapter shows how we found our first coaches and clients, as well as how we set out to engage and work with women. 'We are looking for volunteers to coach female prisoners at HMP Styal near Manchester Airport. This will be very challenging but could also change the lives of all concerned.' I did not plan to set up a charity. I meant to work alone. Yet this idea attracted immediate and increasingly wide support wherever I mentioned it – to strangers on trains or friends in bars. I found no other organization coaching in this way in 2010 and a dozen people replied when I emailed the request above to a hundred or so contacts and two e-newsletters. People continue to get in touch through word of mouth, despite never advertising again, and over 25 coaches have now worked for CIAO.

Of the first 12 coaches a mere quarter had both coached and worked in a prison in any capacity. Another quarter had never coached and a third were new to criminal justice. Most had a focus on business performance, rather than life in general, although 'life' creeps into high-flying executives' worlds too. I trusted the coaches' skills and approach would adapt and develop. Indeed, the one person who had neither coached nor set foot in a prison became our lynchpin, coordinating all our work in Styal.

Everyone involved worked without payment at the start because we all believed in the potential of human beings to grow and change, both themselves and the communities in which we all live. Coaches agree to take on clients as and when they find time in their busy lives. This was essential as it was everyone's jobs and businesses that enabled us to do this then. Many coaches have stepped back for a while to focus on their family or work, and most return as soon as they can. We designed our flexible model to fit in with this and the benefits of the diversity of a large group of coaches are enormous, though it did add to the complexity. Seeing how coaching helped our clients and their families kept us going through the tough times.

We are not purely altruistic either. I coach for a much more selfish reason too. It is the most fascinating, challenging, hilarious and life-affirming work I have ever done. CIAO had a life-changing effect on many of the coaches, let alone our clients. We learnt good and bad things about ourselves, others and the criminal justice system. The impact was far greater than I ever dreamt when I first drafted that ad over four years ago.

'I hadn't realized how complicated it was.' Coaching in a secure environment can be overwhelming, as the coach who said that implied. We have documents full of useful information, guidance, checklists and ideas on how to do the actual coaching and get the best from your client and yourself. This is in addition to the whole prison experience and the increased risk we might break the law ourselves by going in at all, such as if a mobile phone slips unnoticed to the bottom of a bag, instead of being left in a car.

'It's a lot to take in and you're terrified and proving yourself.' Those were the words of a coach, not a client. We take people into Styal beforehand to get a sense of the place, the risks and the reality of working behind bars. Many were indeed terrified going under the razor-wire slinky for the first time but could then say:

> I thought it would be oppressive but even on the wing it wasn't without hope. To meet women who were able to say just how much the coaching had impacted on the way they were living their lives, how it had given them confidence to change such fundamental things about themselves was inspirational.

New coaches once worked in a group at first, as this was as near as we could get to shadowing or observing one-to-one sessions. Now coaches new to CIAO watch an introductory session for clients and then go in with an experienced 'buddy' who ensures everything runs as smoothly as possible before and after the first time they coach. Reports back demonstrate both the challenges and silver linings coaches are adept at seeing:

> In some ways our prison visit was perfect in that we encountered most of the difficulties that arise when trying to see a client. If it had all gone swimmingly it wouldn't have been anywhere near as useful...It is actually a good thing when things don't all go to plan on a new coach's first client visit. It gives us a chance to discuss how to deal with these things as well as demonstrating the fact that you never know quite what is going to be happening any time you go in.

Once they have mastered the art of sitting down opposite a client in the right place at roughly the agreed time, then coaches can take on other clients. This is not any reflection on their coaching experience, but an acknowledgement of the many additional challenges of coaching behind bars.

Introductory sessions give new coaches a sense of how coaches and prisoners interact. Coaches also see prospective clients and are often paired up with someone from that session too, which helps the chemistry of our loose matching process. Sentence lengths and individual coaches' preferences matter, as clients can have days, weeks, months or years left to serve. The majority of women in all prisons are inside for less than six months and only about 20 per cent have committed violent or serious crimes. Less than a month is much less common – however, sentences of a matter of days are not unheard of. When we began coaching more of our clients were in 'for a while', as lifers are often described, because it was easier for the prison to be sure they would be around long enough for us to coach them. The other upside of this was that it gave us our long-term 'Coaching Champions' for the future. What you are not allowed to do is get a sentence wrong. As a client said, hers was: 'Not nine months! Eight and a half months!!' Every single day counts.

It never occurred to me not to welcome male coaches from the start, but we do ask if clients would be happy to be coached by either a man or a woman. You will note we do not ask which they would prefer, just whether they would be okay with either. CIAO changes lives in many ways but we are not a dating agency. I ran our first ever introductory session with a man and at the end of it asked the group of eight women about being coached by a man or a woman. There were lots of noises along the lines of: 'I don't mind, me' and the occasional 'Ooh. I'd like a man, please!' However, while the other coach was doing something else, one of the women pointed at me, pointed at herself and nodded. I grinned back at her and said that she and I would start the coaching together as soon as possible. That woman was Rebecca. Our first ever client.

First find your client

Our clients are all ages, sentence lengths and offences. To make coaching as accessible as possible, our only criteria are that clients are well, willing, and not violent towards staff. The prison initially estimated 15–20 women might be ready to engage. We now believe over 40 per cent of prisoners in Styal may be coachable – 10 times as many.

Clients were only selected by staff for the first three months, then we rapidly expanded to work with women referred from across the prison. Word of mouth has promoted the service from our very first client onwards, showing the value many place on it. Now almost all our clients put themselves forward after seeing posters or talking to women who had been coached. Some clients became formal 'Coaching Champions' and have an enormous effect encouraging others to sign up.

Clients being well enough to be coached is essential, as well as being sober enough to think with their head 'in the right place'. I often had to work hard to get one client 'in the room' because of her drug use and that very phrase became our trigger for bringing her focus back to coaching. Initially, prison healthcare assessed women's fitness to ensure they were not struggling with identified mental health needs at a level that required specialist help. Just 3 per cent were deemed unsuitable. We now screen those who put themselves forward and support coaches to ensure clients are really in a position to benefit from coaching at this time. Lower-level mental health problems such as depression alone are not necessarily reasons for exclusion, otherwise we could not coach the majority of women in Styal. One client said she appreciated coaching because 'I suffer from depression, so I needed to be able to deal with the here and now and the future rather than the past.'

Many of CIAO's coaches are also trained counsellors and mentors, so we know different approaches are valuable and that coaching can be complementary to these. Indeed, some women do counselling and coaching at the same time. However, many clients in the prison are clear that coaching was best for them: 'It's better than counselling: you're not going through things over and over again. You can see light at the end of the tunnel. I can see the way ahead now.'

One risk CIAO is absolutely not willing to take is coaches being likely to be harmed. Clients must have no recent history of violence nor be a current risk to staff. However, clients' offences can be anything from shoplifting to the most extreme types of murder. Serious offences on their own are no reason to exclude clients from coaching, nor is their being disruptive in the prison. We have therefore worked with long-term prisoners and those on very short sentences with just a few weeks left inside. The majority of women we have coached live in the houses, although I have coached on the wing where prisoners who pose a higher security risk and are more likely to be violent are held, and other experienced coaches have worked with clients from there too. Initially we agreed we would not work with women who were 'disruptive', which was probably to do with risk-management to protect the new coaches. However, we soon changed this to 'not violent', as we strongly believe coaching can get to the root of why someone is being disruptive, so it made more sense to include them.

The only other crucial thing is that our clients are ready to change something, are willing to be coached and realize it is their choice whether or not to take the opportunity. When CIAO was invited to have a stall at

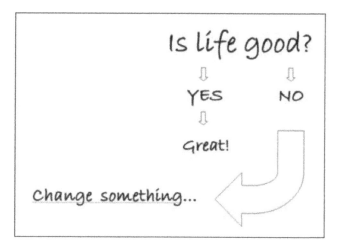

Figure 3.1   Is life good?

a Black History Month event in Styal gym one afternoon we adapted the simple flow chart shown in Figure 3.1 from Gustavo Vieira-Dias to start a conversation about whether women wanted coaching. After a 'catwalk' display of international costumes with more attitude than Paris or New York we simply asked women: 'Is life good?'

That between a half and a third of the women said 'Yes' shocked me. This response reminded me of the reality and normality of prison life for many women, as well as our role in Styal. We are not there to judge, nor to 'rescue', nor to presume. We are simply there to help anyone who wants to change their life to do so. Someone hopefully pointed out perhaps some had already decided to change their life and move forward positively. It later occurred to me it would have been very depressing if everyone had said 'No', as we did not have the capacity to coach everyone we spoke to anyway. There is always a silver lining.

Some women do not realize or feel they can say no if a member of staff suggests coaching. It can be easier to turn up and not engage than to decline the offer up front. Introductory sessions aim to counteract this and help women make an informed decision, as prospective clients have time to explore coaching and fit it into their own mental map, so it makes more sense and they are engaged from the start. As a client said: 'They've got to want to change – it gives you the tools but you have to fix it. It's a two-way thing.' A coaching simulation helps people understand what it is like and explore how it has helped others and how it might help them. They hear it straight from one of our Champions who says: 'it helps you find your own answers'. There is no hard sell. You see the attitude change over the hour as arms uncross and people lean in. A client happily reported back that the coaches said: 'We're not going to tell you what to do because we don't know.' This is crucial, as prisoners had previously said: 'Why are posh people coming in? What are they going to do and teach us? What do they know what it's like?'

Thinking 'What can it do for me?' is a way of operating and surviving inside. Some may start thinking they will go through the motions to help them get early release 'on tag' (i.e. the electronic ankle cuff offenders wear during Home Detention Curfew) but then realize the deeper benefits of personal growth and understanding. Others were clear they did not want to be coached once they saw a 'tag' was not guaranteed. Previous clients tell them it is tough and you have to do real work both during and between sessions but it is 'worth giving up precious free time for'. We stress coaching is not a quick way out of Styal, but a way of achieving so much more. With coaching you are up against yourself, not the system.

We are very aware we are in a controlled and controlling environment and we work hard to ensure there really is a choice to participate. Nor should coaching be done to put a tick in a box nor to please anyone. Not being coached should not count against a client nor lead to any punishment. Using the 'stick' of putting coaching on a formal list of 'things to do' generally reduces willingness to engage. I am always curious who has asked for coaching and who has been 'volunteered'. If it is the latter, it often confirms what the body language shouts from the start. If a client does not want to continue we can simply note 'coaching was not suitable at this point'. As one said:

> There's nothing lost and you're not thought of any differently if you don't want to do it...When you go for that introductory session there's no pressure. It's: 'This is what we could offer. This is what *you* could do for you, not what *we* could do for you. What *you* could do.' I think that's quite important to people.

There can be a big difference between being willing and being ready. An ex-prisoner in Styal said women might think: '"Oh I'd like a bit of coaching." When they're nowhere near it.' We gauge this and often give clients the benefit of the doubt. Feelings can shift too: 'I remember [my coach] saying..."you were a really angry person when you first came in", because I didn't know what it was, or who had put me in for it. I sat there, very reluctant.' This client later sang the praises of her coaching experience to a researcher.

Professional clients have this same range of responses, including a reticence to take up coaching that 'will do you good'. Whether the third party doing the telling is someone who recommends your pay rise or someone who recommends your release from prison makes little difference: well informed volunteers make the best clients. How coaching is viewed and described sits very uneasily with some, perhaps because of its abstract description and occasional use as a corrective tool in business, rather than as a positive way of achieving even more. A number of professional clients have only really been happy for me to coach them when I have called it something else, which I have been happy to do with a smile. Professionals often have significant lead-in times too, as they work out what coaching is, and sometimes an event triggers a specific need or goal for it. Clients in Styal do not have this luxury. This increases the risk of the timing not being right but that is a risk well worth taking for CIAO.

The reward for that risk was clear to new coaches I was showing around one day. We had stopped to chat about coaching with a small group of prisoners and, after I had explained what it was, a previous client walked past and simply said: 'Do it. You'll never know how big an impact it has.'

Rebecca

I waited over an hour, alone in a 'legal visits' room on the warm Sunday afternoon of 14 March 2011. A table and two chairs shared the tiny space on which the high, narrow window did its best not to shed any light. The joy and pain of families briefly reunited rebounded off the door to the main hall.

Rebecca burst in. All apologies and damp hair. You make the most of whenever you are allowed a shower in Styal. She had rushed from her house, with conditioner still in, the moment she heard I was here. It was a great start. We settled down, looked at where she was now and began talking about relationships and accommodation on release. It was clear things were not quite right, as she had hidden the part of her life relating to her offence from her partner. However, rather than delving into this, I made the tiniest of pencil notes and let her lead where she wanted.

When we met again four days later I asked if she wanted to explore that at all. She completely stunned me by saying she had written a confession to her partner the very next day and he had replied immediately to say he already knew.

> It lifted a great weight off my shoulders . . . the hiding caused me loads of depression and stress. I had a broken-down relationship. It was because I couldn't be honest . . . Thinking back, it's weird. It took all these years and it took me one session and I wrote a letter.

Rebecca happily admitted she was highly doubtful coaching could achieve anything:

> At first I thought: 'How's anything going to change?' But I started to feel better about myself and I don't know why. The prison is giving me a second chance...I don't want to be in a rut any more, but it's hard...If anyone's gonna change anything it's gotta be me. I'm so glad I started on these sessions...You ask all the right questions and get me thinking.

Coaching did more than just get her thinking. Rebecca proudly told me she had three Green Tickets for good behaviour in just two weeks, whereas she 'had loads of Red Tickets in the past'. More importantly, she was assessed and approved for early release on a Home Detention Curfew (HDC) 'tag'. This meant she was with her children again within weeks of meeting me and she said: 'I think [coaching] was the reason I got HDC.'

This was my very first experience of coaching behind bars and it has never ceased to amaze me since. I learnt many invaluable lessons from my six hours with Rebecca over four sessions in under four weeks – the most important of which was not to get too cocky in Styal. When we discussed role models I asked if she admired anyone. She went silent for a while before looking at me and saying: 'I admire you.' I had just started to puff myself up a little and wipe a small tear from my eye when she coolly added: 'I wish I were dead full of myself.'

Starting coaching properly

That whirlwind description of my work with Rebecca captures how we started coaching at speed when, despite careful plans to sign up clients inside for a while, it transpired she might be out in under a month. This was just the first of many 'emergency' clients triggered by the short stays in Styal. My favourite such request remains: 'Is anyone able to coach a client due to give birth in a couple of months who will probably be released shortly afterwards?' I literally ended up holding that baby.

Meanwhile, our formal plan meant I began working with another client and three other coaches took on two clients each. The four of us paired up, with each couple including a coach who had worked in prisons before. We then used all our experience to help us explore and share what we learnt with our fellow pioneer. What follows is the more measured approach of the organization we then called Coaching with Styal and now call CIAO.

Hello...Who are you? You are in a prison about to walk into a room to coach. The sum total of what you know for sure is your client's prison number, which you have carefully written down, and her name, which you memorized before the paper began to self-destruct. Mission impossible? More to the point, imagine you are a prisoner about to walk into a room to 'be coached' by a complete stranger and have no real idea what that means. It is amazing anyone turns up.

Coaches are deliberately told very little about their client. We do not even know what she has done. Looking on the internet is never a good idea nor a good source of the truth either, as one of my clients said about the gossip around a newly arrived prisoner: 'I remember what they said about me on the news. I came across as a complete psycho.' Coaches can ask not to coach women who have committed the most extreme crimes. However, so far not one coach has stepped back from anything. We are all there for everyone.

At the beginning we coached all over the prison: in the dining room or sitting room of houses (with other prisoners regularly breezing in and apologizing when they saw us), on the mother and baby unit (with a baby asleep in a pushchair alongside), on the wing (on chairs down the centre, in a cell or in a semi-transparent cube at one end), in the chapel, in the resettlement centre and on benches outside when the sun shone. The disjunction could not be starker with the plate-glass corporate offices coaches are commonly thought to frequent. I have even coached talking through an observation flap in a cell door. Fortunately, the prison has now given us the luxury of two small rooms of our own.

People know where we are too, whereas we might have quietly sat down for a session in any empty room in the past. This opportunistic approach worked well for coaching but less well for security. Being just one number out on the head count of a 'stand-fast roll check' can be the difference between a smoothly running establishment and very unwelcome news headlines. Thinking someone might have escaped when she is actually thinking quietly in a room with her coach is not a good thing, so our new location was welcomed by everyone.

Hello... Where are you? To get as far as facing your client was once something of a miracle and one we work hard with staff to make commonplace. It may surprise those unfamiliar with prisons that it is not always easy to get in through the gate, let alone find the person you came all that distance to see. Such challenges have meant some of us have developed the patience of saints and some of us are amazed simply to have become patient.

Finding appointment times and finding clients used to be like playing 'battleships'. Tracking someone down can be time intensive as coaches do not have their mobiles in prison and not everyone has a two-way radio. It is particularly frustrating to know a client is within 250 metres, but you do not know in which direction. Equally she might have been 'shipped out' that morning and now be in a prison 250 miles away. One snapshot showed about 1 in 10 clients who said they wanted to be coached did not turn up and a similar number were unable to, due to just such a transfer.

We stress the client's responsibility for prioritizing appointments to ensure attendance wherever possible but family or legal visits, dentist appointments and so on do happen and even professional clients cancel. Both sets of clients can also find it hard to summon up the will to attend because 'it's hard work'. Less common among professionals is finding out the venue has been quarantined, as when there was an outbreak of mumps and chicken pox on the mother and baby unit.

We double the chance of at least seeing someone by booking two clients or more for any one trip. This was particularly important as some coaches travel a long way to get to the prison. Coaching two at a time also helps new coaches avoid human nature's trap of thinking their client is a 'typical' Styal woman. Cancelling with enough warning is much better than making a long journey, getting in through the gate and only then finding out the session will not happen after half an hour of searching. At one point I started anticipating cancellations and not planning for sessions because preparing and not using the thinking fresh in my mind destroyed me a little. My patience in these circumstances was greatly helped by cycling to the prison (hence occasional shouts of: 'Miss! Miss! Your backside's wet!'). At least I manage to get some exercise, whatever happens. Let us be as positive as ever and assume all has gone smoothly.

Hello? We took ages discussing how to introduce ourselves without revealing personal information. In the Real World we share who we are with clients or even justify who we are to some. Then we had the brainwave that we could just say something like: 'Hello, I'm Clare, your coach, and I'm really looking forward to working with you.'

Sharing things about yourself can help build rapport but we were very wary of what level to share at. We had been told to consider: 'What could be your painful triggers? What could compromise or be used against you? What are the skeletons in your closet?' It turned out coaches were rarely asked personal questions and deliberately not revealing information did not feel unnatural, as some feared. You can say how you are and share elements of your life that are emotional rather than factual without feeling you are holding back. Indeed, if a client starts asking about the coach this can be a warning signal. Should the coaching be over, if the client's focus has moved away from themselves, are they distracted, or is there another reason for this deflection?

In the end I had done more than 20 sessions before a client even asked how I was, let alone who I was. It really took me by surprise. A startled face followed by laughter is not generally my response to such a friendly question.

Great expectations

Congratulations. You made it in, found your client, smiled warmly at them and earned the right to do a small amount of admin. This ticks a few boxes and gives you both time to settle in and get a sense of who you are talking to; as an ex-prisoner explained: 'Their guards are up. They're defensive.' Agreeing the ground rules clients and coaches commit to is the core of this, with the words on paper reinforced by coaches' body language. Ground rules also give us permission to coach the client and explore the innermost thoughts and feelings they may not even realize they have yet. Asking is particularly important in prison, as it gives back some control in an environment where people's permission is not always sought.

At the heart of our commitment is wanting the very best for every single one of our clients: not the best for the system, but the best for them as people. We have high expectations for them and this is appreciated. It only really struck me how unusual this might be in a prison when a client said in amazement: 'Thank you very much!' Has anyone ever had more faith in you than you had in yourself? It has happened to me many times and repeatedly helped make me realize I could do far more than I thought.

This positive approach links with our neither judging nor comparing them to others. A coach's role is to help clients get the best out of themselves and complete honesty is required from both sides for that. While we encourage honesty and openness we do have limits to our confidentiality. If we believe there is any risk a client might harm herself or be a risk of harm to others then we tell a member of staff as soon as possible. We were told 'keep your dial at "normal"' as to whether or not someone needs support, rather than assuming the prison has higher thresholds before it helps people. Coaching can also stir up distressing emotions or issues which cannot be resolved within the session, particularly if you uncover subjects not spoken about before. This is why we ask every client who they can talk to about what has happened afterwards. Answers have included staff and fellow prisoners but my favourite was 'Jeremy Kyle'.

Coaching can mean a fundamental shift in thinking and it was not just Rebecca who was dubious about what it could achieve. We offer our six hours flexibly over the number of sessions that suits client and coach. Sessions are generally about three weeks apart but this varies too. A coach herself said: 'Before I started I thought: "What difference could we possibly make in six hours?"' and I see her point. Our clients include young people in their late teens and some in their sixties. During however many years they have been alive they have often suffered unthinkable pain and some have inflicted it. They have also developed their own ways of coping with life, as we all do. Those approaches may not be working well for them or, indeed, for our communities as a whole. So, what can anyone possibly do in six hours to counteract all that has gone before, let alone a complete stranger?

What we do is we start right where the client is by asking: 'What do you want to change?' The next chapter shows how we break this down into bite-size chunks but, before then, here is another glimpse of the possibilities inherent in coaching.

Alex

Once the client and coach have both put their first names at the top of the ground rules, we have permission to coach the client and can ask huge questions like 'What do you want from life?' Although I tend to soften it at the start to: 'What do you want from coaching?' This question is often still enough to stop people in their tracks. The simplest answer I have ever had was one word that made me freeze... 'Hope'. I took a deep breath as I looked back into Alex's eyes. The eyes of someone who had no hope at all.

Months later I was showing some new coaches around the wing when I randomly chose a cell to ask if we could have a look inside and saw it belonged to Alex. She invited us in and happily answered the others' questions about what life was like in the prison. After a while I asked how she was, now someone else had coached her. I could scarcely believe the reply from someone who had previously looked so full of fight and yet so utterly crushed: 'It took time to process, but now I'm full of hope.' I smiled in delight and astonishment and if Alex were the hugging type she would have got a bear hug. That is what we can do through the power of coaching. That is the difference we can make in less than six hours. We can unlock hope.

4   What do you want to change?

If you're lucky then you know what you want to change in life and a coach can help you think that through. However, clients are often unsure where to start and a few realize what they thought was the problem is just one of the symptoms. This is how we help our clients look at their lives as a whole and then support them in defining the best goals for them.

What do *you* want? Think about it. What do you *really* want? This vast question is essential to how we all live our lives, yet a coach effectively asks it within minutes of meeting a prisoner. A new client, like most of us, has generally never thought that deeply before. The answers can be extraordinary in different ways: 'Clarity', 'To find out who I really am', 'To change my behaviour and the way I think', and 'Everyone gets to die but not everyone gets to live. I feel like I'm just existing. I want more.'

This mirrors professional clients I work with, in that half know exactly what they want to change but not how to change it, and the other half have no idea: they just know they want to change something. The element that is very different is few professionals have almost given up completely on life itself: 'I didn't know what I wanted to know or do – I was dead inside.'

What we want from coaching

CIAO wants to create lifelong change. What we do not aim to do is reduce crime. This is for the same reason we do not call our clients 'offenders', other than to explain with whom we work to others. This encourages a radical mental shift. We absolutely do want people to stop offending: for their sakes and for the sake of others and our communities. Our aim goes beyond that though. We want people to reach their potential, whatever that may be. We did not want our goal to be a negative one. It would weaken the power and possibilities if we only aimed to stop people offending. The whole point is that coaching both frees and challenges each individual to explore and prioritize what *they* really want to change in their lives. Keeping our aims separate from the criminal justice system is essential. Our independent approach promotes trust and the level of engagement transforms how we can work with clients.

We are confident coaching can help stop people committing crime though, and someone in probation told me of clients who now:

> had a firm idea as to where their futures lay. This confidence and evidence of planning will certainly have helped as it shows positive steps by the individual to address their risk...of offending and risk of harm.

Our 'Theory of Change' behind coaching's impact

CIAO's clients want to change something about themselves or their lives, although they are not always sure what and are frequently unsure how.

↓

Coaching helps them to work out their own aims and values, so they can come up with solutions and actions that work best for them.

↓

It then supports them to achieve those aims and explores any challenges, setbacks, self-limiting assumptions or behaviour along the way.

↓

This helps them to achieve or move towards their goals and increase their understanding of themselves and others.

↓

This achievement builds self-esteem, self-reliance, and the ability to consolidate and achieve further change for themselves.

↓

This in turn this has a positive impact on those around them, not least their children and potential victims.

Coaching is iconoclastic, a form of reflective intervention largely as alien to staff as it is to prisoners. It gives power, confidence and independence to make positive changes. If you can influence people to manage themselves in an environment where adult responsibility is largely removed, then they have that skill for life.

Astrology: the Outcomes Star

To help clients consider life as a whole we break it down into themes, rather than starting with the thing uppermost in their minds or, commonly in prison, what they think you want to hear. I generally ask professional clients to tell me what I need to know in order to coach them. In prison this risks a focus on painful pasts or the offence the person is being punished for, from which we want to move on.

This is why the Outcomes Star tool is at the heart of the first session. It shows the big picture, it looks at key themes in life and stimulates thinking, as well as supporting and measuring change. We used the original Homelessness Star, which gives a clear structure for exploring aspects of the client's current situation with headings such as motivation, money and health. Even when you are in prison you still need to manage your finances, relationships and accommodation. These points are also similar to the government's 'reducing reoffending pathways' – i.e. areas known to promote 'desistance' from crime. The Star shown in Figure 4.1 shows the average initial results for our early clients in the inner ring.

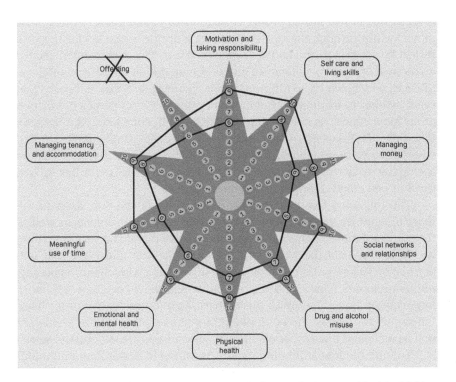

Figure 4.1 Average Outcomes Star scores (before and after coaching) in 2011
© Triangle Consulting Social Enterprise. See www.outcomesstar.org.uk

The larger outer ring is where they were at the end of their coaching. Reviewing the Star once coaching is over helps explore, illustrate and celebrate progress. It can also really surprise our clients, as you will see later.

The Star helps clients assess for themselves which areas they want to change, instead of someone else assessing them. The focus is on exploring the reality of their life, not diagnosis. However, the 'score' is a useful term outside the sessions and this is facilitated by a colour-coded scale of 1–10. The top score of 10 is where clients are self-sufficient and do not feel in need of any help. Detailed descriptions for each point help the client gauge which best reflects their situation. This means the scores are neither guesswork nor 'pick a number, any number...' This increases consistency and counteracts change in moods or interpretation. The coach might support or challenge by asking for examples or 'evidence' behind scores, but the final decision is the client's.

Clients choose where they want to begin. Most of mine simply start at the top with 'Motivation and taking responsibility', although, as this is the most abstract, some clients choose elsewhere. Others tackle the area that presents the greatest challenge, while some deliberately leave that till last. If some points feel less appropriate to a client's situation it is possible to move swiftly through those. Some clients score the same ladder twice to reflect how it is in prison and in their life outside. This is particularly so for areas such as 'Managing tenancy and accommodation' and 'Meaningful use of time', which can be so different inside. Some split 'Social networks and relationships' to distinguish family from others. If a lot comes out or you are a 'slow coach', as one among us calls herself, completing the Star can take time. If it takes more than one session the client simply thinks back to where they were previously. Discussing the different positive aspects and seeing the results on paper helps build a picture. As a client said: 'Looking at the Star you could clearly see the problem areas.'

The following two chapters use the themes of the Star itself to tell more of what we learnt about the underlying pain and problems as well as the many solutions clients came up with to solve them. The very first thing we do is cross out the word 'Offending' on the Star and leave that ladder blank. This stresses our philosophy of working with clients as people, not as prisoners. This can transform how they view coaching and, more importantly, how they brand themselves. As another coach put it: 'What I'm saying to them is: I'm not looking at you as a prisoner. I'm looking at you as a client. I have other clients outside and you are exactly the same.'

To look back at offending closes down positive thinking and maintains the label, whereas building on strengths, rather than shoring up weaknesses, can open up a whole new world of previously unimagined possibilities.

Some people are very uncomfortable speaking about it because at the end of the day they've been to court, they've been judged and now they're being punished and they don't want to go over all things like that, so I think for them to say that at the start is really refreshing.

It can still be hard to avoid coaching related to a client's offending. It once took me 10 hours to realize I had worked on a goal of 'going straight'. This was linked to 'keeping clean' and off drugs, but it still made me smile that such a fundamental error passed me by.

Clients can tell you their offence, even if you say you neither want nor need to know, and this can help illuminate where they are mentally and emotionally. However, the coach has to be careful not to ask questions out of personal curiosity, rather than questions that will help the client move forward. If it feels like you have spent a little too long looking back then you probably have. Letting things out can be essential though: 'My client said, "I've done something terrible." She really needed to tell me and once she had we were both able to breathe normally again, to say, "That's out now" and move forward.' Others take longer before saying it, as they cannot quite believe we're really not curious about it:

My coach was more interested in me than what I was here for and I'm thinking ee my goodness, this is unusual . . . they're going to get to that bit, why I'm here, and I was waiting for it. I was really waiting for it but it never came. It never came. In the finish I told her . . . I ended up telling her, but that was my choice.

Rebecca asked, 'Do you want me to tell you what I've done?' I said no and she immediately told me, because she wanted or even needed to. I can't remember what her crime was now. I will tell you the finest details about how she and I grew through her coaching though. In fact I'm only really sure of what just one of my clients actually did to be sent to prison.

Highs and lows of stargazing

'I've never thought about all these things. It felt good. I enjoyed that!' is in stark contrast to a woman who found it challenging reviewing her situation in this way: 'The first session was a bit gruelling for her: reflecting for the first time.' The Star's clear scale can really help counter low self-esteem though: 'She was surprised at where she was scoring herself e.g. she might randomly and subjectively put herself at 3 but her actual score using the objective scale was 7.'

Low scores give us an opportunity to emphasize the great potential a client has for change. Having some high scores shows them what they are capable of and can be used to explore relationships between the areas and how they might improve and have done so in the past. High scores can also trigger scepticism. I knew a client had made a real breakthrough when she initially scored herself 9 or 10 then revised it to 2 or 3 and said: 'I was stuck'. It is a ladder, not an escalator. The client has to make some effort to move.

One client's lowest area was a 3 for 'Motivation and taking responsibility'. This is probably as low as you can get after you have actually chosen to turn up for coaching. As we looked down at the completed Star I asked: 'So, which of those areas would you like to address first?' She said: 'I don't mind. What do you think?' I couldn't stop myself laughing as I looked back with my eyebrows raised and she laughed at the irony too when I suggested it really might be good for her to prioritize rather than me taking that responsibility for her.

While some coaches find the session uplifting, others have found the first session to be an hour of politeness as clients worked out who was sitting opposite them. It can feel less structured than professional sessions, particularly if you are used to coaching corporate clients. As a coach put it: 'It felt as if it was in danger of feeling like a cosy chat but actually she just needed to talk.' Coaches work flexibly with this, making the most of appropriate opportunities and moments as they arise.

A client on remand (i.e. one of the 20 per cent of women in prison who have not yet been tried and found guilty or not guilty) did not want to tempt fate by completing the Star at all. She felt it would involve thinking about whether she would be released or inside for years. If released immediately then her life would be good, whereas if she stayed in jail she would lose her home and might start taking drugs. Her future was hostage to the outcome, so completing the Star would be unhelpful. As the criminal justice process continued she learnt she was going to be sentenced for manslaughter or murder and eventually got nearly 20 years. As her coach said: 'Working with that uncertainty is very hard.' However, one year into that long sentence she had already become a recovery mentor helping other women in the prison and was working with another coach.

Back down to earth: GROWing

Once the initial elements and stargazing are complete, it is totally up to the client to tailor their approach and set the agenda with their coach. Coaches use their own experience, knowledge and skills to help their client in a way that feels most comfortable and effective for them both. So, in the rest of the book when I say 'we do this' I am speaking generally for all the coaches, rather than prescriptively. The only three essential areas we all aim to help with are: exploring what the client is aiming for (their goals), what matters to them (their values) and what may be holding them back (their limiting assumptions).

There are many models of coaching towards goals and coaches pick their acronym of choice. GROW is the granddaddy of them all and stands for the phases of exploring the client's: Goal, Reality, Options / Opportunities / Obstructions and Will. Moving cleanly through these is rare, as with any client. More 'Reality' creeps in and 'Options' emerge during the session, if not throughout all the sessions. I use my acronyms loosely and sometimes flit between a few frameworks. It is not a simple linear process but what is needed at that time by that person. This undefined space is where the richness of possibilities and learning is at its best, if coach and client can hold that tension.

Inflexible plans rarely fit well with human beings and I learnt early on that what I want has nothing to do with it. I can be highly structured, if you ignore the creative chaos of my desk, and planned to agree three goals in my first ever session in Styal. However, Rebecca wanted to focus on one, work on that, and see where it took us, rather than planning everything out at the start. The client's agenda and all the unknown potential that can unleash were what really mattered. We may have ended our time together without covering all I initially intended, yet we did more than she or I ever hoped.

Goals are key to coaching, as we want clients to move forward purposefully. We also want to help them consider and realize the resources they already have to help them. A client said: 'When you go through those gates you enter a world you have little physical control over.' But, you still have control of your mind.

Goal-setting: rocket science

Once we have the big picture we stress that coaching is not about who you *were*, but who you *are now* and, more importantly, who you *want to be* in future. Then the crucial questions follow: 'What do you want to change?' and 'Where do you want to start?' Goals can be explicit but many are tangential and not named, or even discussed, as Rebecca has already showed. A client's strength, courage and 'permission' can be all that are needed for them to make extraordinary changes. The Star prompts realization, so I have rarely needed additional triggers for goals. However, if someone is still uncertain about what they want, then to help them consider the possibilities in a particular area I might ask what a perfect 10 on the Star would look like and if any of that appealed. It may seem odd but not everyone wants perfection. The same questions later on can strengthen a client's motivation.

The world is full of theoretical and unscientific 'rules' about setting goals. Coaching is basic rocket science: you decide your goal and channel your energy towards it. It is rocket engineering that is really complicated. Rocket science is all about control and using that energy to get precisely where you want to be. Without direction it is simply an uncontrolled explosion that can cause more damage than good.

Some prefer the excitement and unpredictability of a managed explosion. Then you're not waiting for momentum to build and inertia to be overcome but are immediately getting on with something (like starting a coaching service in a prison, for instance) without waiting for people to point out all the reasons why it is impossible. CIAO has not just come about through trial and error; we thought ideas through using the wisdom of groups large and small. I don't always plan everything in detail before starting. Things change, regardless of plans. Refuelling in flight and using boosters to improve my targeting as I go are part of what makes my life worth living. This can unsettle those who choose to join me, but if they hang on they generally find it worthwhile.

Most clients are keener on clean 'rocket science' than my less predictable approach. They also find goal-setting gives them resilience and can make a sustainable change to how they live. Whatever their style, our clients need to find the energy or rocket fuel that a desire to change something gives them. One client chose a different simile: 'It's like driving. Before I was just driving around aimlessly not getting anywhere in particular, but now it's like I have a map so can go straight where I want to.' Navigating through life means taking control, whether making sense of corporate life or a criminal sentence.

Goals are all about motivation and satisfaction. Short-term pain can result in long-term gain but the reality is we only ever live in the present, even if our emotions stem from thinking about the past or the future. Goals mean lifting your head to look at something you want now, as now is all we really have. So goals should improve our life at this moment, whether that improvement comes from anticipation of the result or immediate change. If goals do not do this, then what is the point? Motivation is likely to be hard or nonsensical. If you believe you are hopeless with no chance of change or control then your pain is locked in with you. This is why coaching matters so much in prison where hope can die.

If your goal overwhelms rather than inspires you, you might want to reconsider it or you will never get off the ground. SMART goals, which are Specific, Measurable, Attainable, Realistic and Timely, may work for some, but my goals are for making life bearable or joyful right now, not just long term. This perspective is particularly helpful if you have time to serve or are very aware of death, like me. It also explains why I am happy with my outwardly ridiculous 10-year goal of changing the culture of our society. Working towards that adds meaning to my life and to the pleasure and the pain along the way.

Reality: the raw materials

Once a coach knows the client's goal, we ask if it is appropriate in two senses. Is it within CIAO's remit to coach a client towards that goal? Does the coach feel it is within their skills and personal boundaries to help? CIAO works with clients on anything legal and not connected with them as an offender – i.e. we never coach about appealing a sentence. Legality is not something that has crossed my mind with any professional clients. However, no one has tried to use coaching to become a better criminal either, as far as I am aware.

We explore whether or not a goal is realistic and under the client's control so that: 'Instead of worrying about things I can't do, I'm putting all my energy into things I can affect.' Coaching is both powerful and empowering. Coaches work to increase a client's self-esteem: to realize they have their own answers and can create their own options. We do not raise false hope by saying: 'You can do anything if you set your mind to it.' Although I firmly believe that, while we cannot do whatever we want in life, we can often do far more than we dare to imagine. Life coaches who peddle the unrealistic 'you can be anything you want to be' line or pander to the materialistic promising to help you 'make a million' do not improve how coaching is viewed by many. This can also be seen as self-indulgent therapy for people with more money than sense. Some have rolled their eyes thinking coaching is pink and fluffy but their eyes have widened when they hear what we actually do inside. A prison psychiatric worker who thought it 'airy-fairy' now sees it as highly practical and tough.

Coaches have to hold their nerve and composure when faced with seemingly overwhelming goals, such as Akshata who simply replied: 'I want to overcome this. I don't know where to start and I don't know where I'm going.' That sounds simple enough, but what she meant by 'this' was the death of all her immediate family: the death of her father of prostate cancer, the death of her sister as a result of female circumcision and the death of her mother who died while fleeing with Akshata to protect her from being circumcised. Writing that, I had to take a deep breath, as I did when with her. Coaching behind bars often raises challenges beyond any I have faced in my corporate practice. A very long way beyond. Yet she was in a totally different positive place when she was released just a few months later and we laughed a great deal in between.

Some might think it would be hard to focus with release looming; however nearing release can actually help clients work out things they can put into action more immediately. Equally, our coaching is not just about considering goals for when women leave the prison. We also look at aspects of their lives they want to change while they are inside, as many of our clients are there for some time. If a woman is a long way off leaving it may be hard to connect with the issues she will face outside, so we can switch to three monthly sessions and consider follow-up thereafter. It is totally up to the client and her coach.

Options: how to build your rocket

As coach and client explore the reality, the options, opportunities and/ or obstructions appear. This enlightening phase reveals barriers I never dreamt existed. In turn, clients come up with solutions they never knew possible, sometimes as soon as they articulate the problem, sometimes a lot later. As well as goals prompted by the Star's points and many beyond them, coaches almost always also work on things clients do not initially realize they need or want to change, such as self-esteem. As a consultant I am used to people coming up with solutions as soon as I ask about them, because problem-solving is human nature. In prison there can be a barrier greater than any prison wall – an absolute lack of confidence that clients can do anything to change their lives. This major problem is rarely raised explicitly as a goal but is often painfully visible. This barrier has nothing to do with ability and everything to do with self-belief.

Some coaches have found not suggesting options:

> slightly more difficult in the prison because they lack, or many of the women I talk to lack, the confidence to say, 'Well I could try doing this or I could try doing that.' Whereas in the corporate world, if anything, people are overly confident about how they might achieve a goal and when they might have it sorted by.

Occasionally, clients inside are overconfident too, but you have to be sure this arrogance is not simply a mask. Professionals can be much better at hiding low self-esteem, but are then often relieved to share their belief that 'I'm a fraud' or to work out how to overcome the paralysis of perfectionism.

Coaching unlocks a whole box of tools to address Abraham Maslow's problem that 'it is tempting, if the only tool you have is a hammer, to treat everything as if it were a nail'. People who never realized they had a choice can now choose. Others realize it was bad choices, if very hard ones, that put them inside in the first place:

> It's given me the tools to speak up for myself, to say what I really want... I know I can achieve so much more. But I felt for a lot of my life that... I wasn't worthy of doing anything more so I didn't.

We ask 'What would you like instead?' and encourage clients to try out different ways of responding to situations they are unhappy with.

Coaches help them realize they can choose different behaviours, or even different feelings. We can then support them as they test things out and think through the possible consequences through questioning, role-play or other approaches. Sometimes the time frame of 'What do you want your life to be in five years?' can be far enough away yet soon enough for some issues or clients, while incomprehensible for others. Then more immediate questions like 'What can you do today?' and 'What's the one most important thing to do now / this week / this month?' can work better.

Will: rocket fuel

CIAO helps clients realize they can choose how they respond and then challenge them to take responsibility and be held accountable for their decisions and commitments. If they believe all the fault lies with others they give their power away, so it can shift perception to ask: 'If perhaps less than one per cent might just be down to you, what might that contribution have been?' A client later said 'I blamed everyone for all that had gone wrong in my life and 90 per cent was me.'

Responsibility lies behind the simplest of words. Using the right pronoun means the difference between a client saying 'I choose to do that', and a client speaking for their coach and all humanity in saying, 'You do that, don't you?' A moment of personal triumph was when a client in Styal said something she would take away from coaching was the independence of 'saying "I" not "you" and taking responsibility'. I could have hugged her. In fact, I probably did.

We also help women realize that there are things, like the abuse many have suffered, for which they have no responsibility whatsoever. There are no excuses for much our clients have done, but some of the things that have happened to them are equally inexcusable. We challenge and help many clients to take ownership of change: clients who have been shaped and controlled by others all their lives, such as their families, partners and now those they are imprisoned with. Questions can overcome inertia by showing a client they are capable of change and building momentum: 'Tell me about a change you have made in the past. Walk me through it in detail. What were you thinking, feeling, saying and doing when you decided and acted?'

The prison takes away many choices and coaching gives some fundamental ones back, along with hope. Not the blind hope that the whole world will miraculously change, but that they can change themselves and parts of the world around them. Some explicitly choose to become survivors not victims. We may have free will but most of our behaviour results from nature and nurture. Interventions, such as coaching, that help us use our free will to best effect, can make a huge difference. It can remove the paralysing fear that stopped women moving forward.

Coaches can help clients turn pain into strength: 'You bravely accepted the reality of your situation – even though it hurts – and used that hurt to fuel your determination to change. You discovered that by relying on your inner strength you can allow your outer self to soften.'

We notice and build on clients' internal motivation, as this is what they take away with them. Realization of the possibility of change means a client's motivation has increased from three to five during her first session alone. More vitally, a client can move from wondering about the point of living: 'Before I was thinking dead bad thoughts. I didn't want to do anything' to 'A lot more things have gone good for me since. I did more things and got positive things back. I used to think I could just sit around and wait for good things to happen.'

What is your prime motivator: the avoidance of pain or the pursuit of pleasure? Carrot or stick? What punishment has ever worked for you? We need different flavoured carrots, as we cannot wield a bigger stick than some women are beaten with in other areas of their lives. Prison is not a perfect deterrent. For some it is part of the game. For others it provides both family and sanctuary.

Fortunately, prison is also a place people can learn and develop. Clients have gained more than just insights from coaching. Some have taken the tools themselves: 'I've used the GROW model with other problems... I can use the GROW skill to problem-solve rather than leaving a problem as a bad thing.'

Lift off

Sometimes your client has a revelation about themselves or others that they want to explore immediately and you can barely keep them in the room. More generally, once they know where they want to go and have the belief that they can get there, you work with them to pin that destination down and map out the reality of the journey:

> When I saw it written down on paper I realized that I can do it rather than it just being a mess in my head... I'll continue doing this now for the rest of my life as it has been so useful and makes it seem possible.'

Prescriptions for describing your goal are numerous. Write in the present tense, so it is already real and your subconscious can work towards it. State it in positive terms, as the brain cannot process negatives and what you do not want may not be the same as what you do. Use 'when' not 'if'. Have a realistic but challenging target date and a clearly defined destination that helps you know when you have reached it. Put in as much detail as you can about this 'compelling future' and use all your senses as far as possible. Include the context of where and with whom you will be, etc., etc.

I have used all or none of these with clients in Styal. Even making notes at all can be something of a breakthrough: 'sometimes... it's as simple as them actually writing it down so they know what they've agreed to, whereas previously they never wrote anything down so they'd forget'. Many have enjoyed imagining their future, as it takes them out of their cell and beyond the prison fence. Lynn gave birth in the short gap between two of our coaching sessions and wrote about her life one year on from then. This hand-written description filled me with even more hope for the tiny baby I held.

> I've just finished my first week of my new college course and I'm loving it so far. I've met a few new friends and everybody seems really nice and welcoming. I worried about being the oldest person there but it's a diverse group and I haven't felt one bit uncomfortable and I'm finding it easy to join in conversations so it's doing wonders for my confidence.
>
> The morning routine is taking some getting used to and it's not easy getting a baby and toddler as well as myself ready and out the door on time, but it's getting easier and it's definitely worth it because my days are so full with something I'm enjoying that I'm not sat moping around or feeling bored. My cooking skills are improving and the kids are enjoying the benefits of my labours, especially the cakes. [Two of them] are also getting stuck in with the prep and washing up when I practise at home, though we end up with a lot more mess than necessary, it's all good fun and something we can do together.
>
> When I think back a year ago and I was still in prison wondering where I'd be and what I'd be doing two years from then, I realize how far I've come and how well I'm doing and I'm really proud of myself. I've got what's important to me: a nice house for the kids, who are all settled and happy after the upset of last year, new friends and a college course I'm enjoying. Hopefully this time next year I'll be settled in a job and planning my own little business.

Mission control

My coaching training taught me to be similarly prescriptive about keeping goals alive, so I used to recommend: 'Review them by reading them aloud to yourself daily, first or last thing. This will put them at the front of your conscious mind and help keep them strong as your subconscious works towards them.' Now I help the client explore what works for them.

Most clients see how defining steps along the way helps them know they are getting there and use feedback of all kinds to measure their progress: 'I never thought about planning things before, but now I do as I know it helps to break things up into smaller actions.' Then it is not so overwhelming: 'Before, everything looked too big – I wanted to be at the finish line without taking the first step!' Changing habits can enable us to achieve our goals but there is a reason they are so often described as 'ingrained'. Some clients are helped by anticipating setbacks and how to deal with them, or rewarding themselves by buying treats along the way as an additional incentive if progress becomes slow or tough:

> I feel happier now. I knew I wanted to do things but didn't do them. I can now prioritize and as I've written down what I need to do in the short term it seems achievable so I just do them. I feel good after doing any of my actions as I feel a sense of achievement. Working out my goals helped a great deal segregating them by time, i.e. splitting them into short-, medium- and long-term objectives. It made it realistic and seem possible as I realized that I didn't have to do everything immediately.

Finding the space, time, people and other resources to give you the support infrastructure to achieve your goals can be a lot tougher in prison. However, how others react has helped many clients see which relationships are helping them and which are holding them back. Getting people to leave you alone at times, as well as be there when you need them, is hard inside too. This fills me with even more admiration for the clients who work out their own way forward despite the additional limitations the prison environment brings.

The first explicit goal I worked with a client on was losing weight: a goal that could be linked to so many needs and emotions. I love that Rebecca's first implicit and explicit goals were about taking metaphorical and real weight off her. She asked about weight loss and I told her that she knew the answer, but she carried on looking down. I asked her to look at me, looked directly back and repeated: 'You know the answer to that.' She smiled and told me she knew what she should do and described it in detail. Before her next session she asked the doctor to change the medication which affected her weight, cut down on sugar and ordered sweeteners, gave up working on the servery where she ate too much, and was losing pounds before she had even started exercising. 'I feel better about myself. I've had no chocolate all week. I've not even thought about it.'

You see, it is rocket science. It is about the energy and direction you have when you reach for the stars. NASA are not the only ones who know the secrets of success. Women in Styal are the experts when it comes to their own lives too: yet another thing they have in common with us all.

5 The pain

The three parallel cuts on Sarah's arm looked as if a lion had swiped at her. This outward sign of inner pain at seeing her children just twice in six months could not be clearer. Her feelings of worthlessness meant she did not believe she could be a good mother after trying to kill herself.

This and the next chapter get to the heart of what we have seen and heard behind bars. Some of this hits hard but none of it is completely without hope, even for Sarah – in fact, particularly for Sarah and for her children. This chapter looks at how prison affects your emotions and mental well-being, as well as the relationships past and present, inside and out, that underpin those.

Sarah had used alcohol to cope with her uncle abusing her from the age of 14, then found out her partner was unfaithful soon after her third child was born. Drunk, suicidal and alone in a semi-detached house, she smashed her own reflection in a mirror and used a shard of the glass to slit her wrists. Then she committed arson by setting light to a rug on the sofa, turned the gas on and took photographs of her children upstairs with her. She lay down in the bath, turned on the taps and waited to die as the fire took hold.

Her guilt at this and how she had betrayed her children by not feeling able to continue living for them was overwhelming. How Sarah and I addressed the limiting beliefs that preceded and followed on from this is described in Chapter 9. Coaching had as great an impact on her children as it had on her: they now know just how much she loves them and their lives are brighter for it. Months later she said: 'If I'd had coaching earlier I think it would have stopped me coming to prison. I think it would have saved my life. It has saved my life. I've not cut myself since that first group session.'

Our approach may be identical to my work with all my clients, yet the context and painful extremes of some prisoners' lives create fundamental challenges. I have never worried about any professionals walking out in a suicidal state or returning home to a deeply damaging personal relationship. There has been unhappiness but nothing gets near what I have seen in Styal.

Emotional and mental health – what makes life worth living?

On sunny days, bare arms covered with the straw of criss-crossing scars stand testimony. I am glad I only ever heard about, rather than met, a woman who 'bites through her arm until the artery is exposed' and another who 'has pushed a razor blade three inches up into the flesh under a cut'. A client showing me the staples holding the flesh of her arm together and other more open cuts she had made was more than enough. Another client was late as she could not dry her own hair because of her slashed wrists, and a friend had to do it for her.

My own wounds over the years make me dispassionate about blood and stitches, but mine were accidents. My stapled client wrote: 'I need 2 get back on track + find better 'n' more sensible ways 2 deal with my emotions.' This made it even more poignant when I later asked what brought her joy and she said: 'knowing I've not cut up in a while', adding, 'I've found better ways to manage my anger'.

The psychology of self-harm is complex and varied. Cutting, scouring with a harsh cleaning pad and other forms of damage women inflict on themselves can be 'coping mechanisms' or a way of feeling 'alive'. Self-harm is often a symptom of hidden distress and some people talk of causing a physical pain that equals and externalizes their invisible internal anguish. Food refusals can be another way of exerting control. The impact on those around them is high too: women can fight anyone who intervenes to stop them. If staff feel there is a risk of self-harm or suicide, women can be put on 'constant observations' or 'watches'.

If you pick a prisoner at random there is only a 1 in 10 chance they would *not* have a mental health problem. The majority suffer from depression or anxiety, while more severe illness such as psychosis haunts a small but significant number. It was during my years as a trustee of the Revolving Doors Agency that I learnt most about the links between crime, multiple problems and poor mental health. Statistics are overwhelmingly worse inside than out, and worse for women than for men. More than twice the number of women prisoners were assessed with anxiety and depression – nearly 1 in 2 compared with 1 in 5 of the female UK population.

The only time I felt sick with terror at Styal was the day I arrived as an ambulance sped away. All I could think was: 'Is she alive?' and 'Do I know her?' Suicide is an ever-present spectre. Illness, intertwined with fear, mental pain, guilt or soul-destroying remorse, can be fatal. Six women died in Styal in 2003/4 and in just one day six people were 'cut down' 27 times between them after attempts to hang themselves. A coach, who was suitably qualified, offered counselling rather than a coaching session when her client's next-door neighbour had tried to commit suicide that morning: she 'was very angry and upset, her feelings exacerbated by previous experiences of suicide, including one where she was involved in cutting down a friend who had hanged herself [and who had died]'. Thankfully no one has killed themselves in Styal since 2009 and the number of women supported by prison staff because they are 'at risk' of self-harm or suicide is at its lowest ever.

As a prisoner you have to live with the consequences of your own pain and the pain you have caused others. Through coaching we may give prisoners a chance to change all they can in terms of both their perception and the reality. If women in Styal want to change their lives they are often starting from a very low point and need all the hope, motivation, challenge and support they can get to do so. We do not log how many say they explicitly want to work on their mental health, but almost all my clients want to improve it directly or tangentially. Mental health weaves its way into all areas of our lives. The complexity of how the factors interact works both ways, and mental health is key. As so many clients have realized, you work on one area and others improve too.

> Although I'd never, ever wanted to kill myself they were the thoughts that I couldn't rid myself of. I just couldn't. And without [coaching] I don't think I would have had the focus to carry on for the whole nine months. So it has been a bit of a life-saver for me, quite literally.
>
> [It] can be effective in preventing reoffending for those who might reoffend; and for those [like me] who wouldn't anyway, it can make us not want to die.

We are very clear we are not medics. What we can do is help people realize their inner strength. As one coach said:

> I cannot do for her what a trained psychiatrist or counsellor could ... But I can help her work out before she's released how she can look at her future and work out what life will really be like.

For some clients this is what they need: 'Chloe valued the addiction support in the prison but felt coaching had given her far more than medical or psychiatric assistance in relation to her mental health issues.' Wondering if I was getting above myself, thinking coaching really could improve mental health, I rang a professor of psychiatry. He confirmed that many coaches embed practices similar to those you see in cognitive behavioural therapy (CBT) and motivational interviewing: 'It's interesting. You're coming at it from a different perspective and have come up with similar things.'

When a client feels they have failed as a person and are full of self-disgust, instead of self-esteem, it is very powerful to focus on their strengths, their assets, and tap into the ideas and techniques of 'positive psychology' rooted in common humanity. Coaching gives prisoners a degree of control and choice in their lives where simple mind-saving things like going for a walk or calling a friend can be impossible. Coaches also provide an opportunity to talk and be heard while, critically, pushing and helping our clients to move forward. Even when you have tried to kill yourself. Even in a prison. Even when you had given up hope. That is what coaching can do for mental health. It is not a panacea but it is up there with aspirin on my list of pain relievers.

Social networks and relationships: the real punishment

Being kept against your will from the people, things and places you love is the worst punishment for most women in prison and most women's crimes have not deprived someone else of the comfort of a loved one. The majority of prisoners in Styal come from Greater Manchester and Merseyside, but our clients have come from North Wales across to Durham, and returned as far south and north as Oxfordshire and central Scotland. There are far fewer women's prisons than men's and none in Wales. The nearest is over an hour's drive south and even further away from many families.

You can only call your family and friends when you are told, and then only if you have credit and wait your turn. There is no guaranteed privacy and any letters you send or receive may be read. Nothing is as immediate as a mobile phone constantly in your pocket or as comforting as someone at your side. Fleeting visits are tough. Singing Christmas carols with women separated from their children and families hit me hard too. The prison's resident ducks may have their brood around them, but even they are picked off one by one by the crows. The chances of survival are pretty slim. This year three ducklings survived, to our joy.

Coaches do not have a completely detached view either, particularly around relationships. Our feelings and issues are often mirrored:

> I have realized how much I have in common with this client, obviously not a criminal record, but: being a mother, wife, holding down a job, feeling put on by my parents, sometimes finding it hard to be open about my feelings, managing difficult conversations and people with intense emotions. I saw myself in many of the situations she described – and I could learn from it.

A few of my clients have been bereaved while inside. One described going to her brother's funeral handcuffed to an officer as she hugged members of her family, with another officer standing behind her at all times. I met one client for the first time just after her grandmother, who brought her up, had died. I met another the day after her friend in the house opposite died, of what later proved to be an aneurysm and brain haemorrhage, after complaining of headaches. Being able to light a candle in the chapel is small consolation in such circumstances.

'If I'd asked for help I'd have been battered all the more'

Coaches regularly hear of rape and abuse, occasionally when sickeningly young and one from the age of 8 months. About half of women inside have a history of domestic abuse and report emotional, physical or sexual abuse as a child – twice that of male prisoners. Perspectives differ on asking for help. One client said: 'If I'd had coaching 15 years ago I wouldn't be inside' – because back then she had no idea she could ask for help. Whereas another said: 'If I'd asked for help I'd have been looked on as weak and battered all the more.' We are very aware though, that while many women in Styal have endured abuse, often in silence, some have also inflicted it.

Working with clients and hearing tales of abuse is not overwhelmingly sad. This is one young woman's response to three hours' coaching over two sessions just 10 days apart.

Em was closed in on herself but opened up physically and metaphorically as we began to explore her life. In our first meeting she told me her uncle had abused her from the age of 12: 'I went straight from being a child to an adult. I missed out on 13 to 25.' She remembers her mother locking her bedroom door from the outside and not understanding why. Now she realizes she was trying to protect her. When Em was 15, and met her much older long-term boyfriend, her mother was protective again and Em wanted to say: 'I lost my virginity to your brother not him.'

Having shared the burden of what her uncle had done and satisfied me and herself that he was not still a risk to others, she left the room six inches taller. Em's initial scores on the Outcomes Star were mainly 3s, 4s or 5s. 'I thought: counselling and all that – it won't work for me. It's proved me wrong... It's been brilliant. Coaching's really helped me.' Shedding that great weight meant she increased her score for 'Motivation and taking responsibility' from 3 to 6 in her first session alone and felt there was no need to address this at all in the second, when she scored a 9. 'It felt good doing things for myself. It felt like I'd achieved something... My house officer is proud of me.'

Em said she did not want to look further with me at what her abusive uncle had done, instead saying she wanted to see if she could have counselling 'for closure'. Then the impact of her new-found self-belief led her to change this to: 'It's him I need to see, not a counsellor. I wanna know: Why? Why me?' Em had started using drugs as a result of her abuse, and continued to suffer abuse in various forms throughout her life, but never told anyone else in the prison about her uncle. Other services in Styal helped her address both the drug use and domestic abuse, but could do nothing about the initial trauma they knew nothing of. After two coaching sessions she agreed I could share her story if it might help others and she then told prison staff, which meant she could receive appropriate support on release. Em also wanted to move on from her poor relationship with her children's father, while remaining friends. After the first session she went to a domestic violence group and 'felt I wasn't alone'. This is so true. Nearly half of women in prison report experiencing domestic abuse at some point.

Em did not need a third session prior to release and her Star scores had doubled to 9s and 10s. Her reflection on this? 'It's mad!' Yet extraordinary things happen when we give them the chance.

Em was released from Styal within a fortnight. She and I were so hopeful. One week later I was gutted to learn she was back in Holloway prison in London. It was a probation officer who reminded me I did not know what long-term impact our time together would have. I have no idea how both sharing her past and planning a positive future might change her life. A life where she can walk into a family gathering every Christmas and face her uncle with her head held high. A life with totally different possibilities for her and her children. I hope so. I really do.

'Mummy's done something wrong'

The cycle of crime and deprivation means coaching can affect future generations in myriad ways. Poor parenting and a family history of offending are major factors in increasing the risk of someone committing crime, as well as having mental health problems. Adult children of imprisoned mothers are more likely to be convicted of a crime than those with imprisoned fathers; hence a coach said her client was 'working hard to regain the trust of her teenage children and turning her life around after a history of drug taking' as she 'wants to illustrate it can be done'.

Talking about a woman's children when she is inside can be extremely distressing, so we tread carefully and watch our client's response. It is undoubtedly the area that causes the most tears in my sessions. One client new to Styal equated the 10 days she had been without her daughter to a drug addict going cold turkey. She decided to use the energy from that pain to move forward and tire herself out through physical activity, so she could regain her appetite and sleep again. Another was distressed being in prison for the first time on her daughter's birthday. Even good news and happy occasions are harder to deal with when you can't celebrate them. Managing problems from prison can be tough on everyone too: 'I'm not serving this sentence. My family is.'

More positively, Em wanted to change her relationship with her two young children:

> I felt nothing but guilt. I felt I needed to put things right. I didn't know what to write at first. I wrote and explained, 'Mummy's done something wrong and this is why I've been away so long.' I got a letter back off them and the kids are made up. I wanted them to know that's what happens when you do wrong things and I want them to know I'll be home soon and I'll be a better mum.

Two-thirds of CIAO's clients are mothers with the traditional average of two children each. Just a quarter of those children are likely to live with their mother on release – i.e. a third of all those born to our clients. Prisoners are more likely to be single parents who are themselves more prone to social isolation and mental health problems. Less than 1 in 10 children whose mothers are in prison are cared for by their fathers. Many will stay with other family members, be 'looked-after children', or be fostered or adopted. One mother was petrified both fathers would knock on the door of her mother who was looking after her children and take them away, split them up and not allow her access.

One child went to live with her grandparents and thought her mother had died. Some women do not allow their children to come to see them and say they are working away. Children rarely stay in their home area, let alone in their own home, even when they are with family members. As carers are generally older it can be harder to persuade them to make the journey, even if financial support might be available. Many prisons are difficult to reach by public transport, although there are occasional buses and trains to Styal with the train station a 10-minute walk away. If they do make it, children can find visiting frightening, with security searches for drugs and other banned items; boring, as adults talk; or confusing, as they are reunited only to be split up again. You can buy refreshments in the visits hall and there is a children's play area with extended three-hour family visits possible, but you still have to say goodbye at the end.

> Visits from family and friends become one of the most important things to you. They keep you going, keeping that link with the real world outside of those gates. Having a visit is the perfect excuse to clean yourself up, to make an effort from the humdrum days. Looking clean and tidy is a way of putting your family's minds at rest – let them see you are doing okay, you are coping in this strange world.

You cannot visit a prisoner unless they agree to see you and they must send a visiting order that allows a social visit to be booked in advance. No conjugal visits are allowed in this country. It is possible to have 'visits' with people in other prisons via prison video links though. Visiting prisoners through the New Bridge Foundation, a charity set up to support those who have no one to visit them, is part of why I created CIAO. This is how I began working one-to-one with prisoners and I still visit one of my first New Bridge clients, who is also now my friend, as we have known each other over a quarter of our lives. So I have an inkling of what visits mean when you are inside.

Born in Styal

We have coached women before and after giving birth. Styal's mother and baby unit exemplifies the generational cycle, as nine women can live there with their children. If a mother's sentence is longer than 18 months the baby does not generally stay with her. What really hits me about the cycle is that occasionally there are mothers who lived there as babies themselves. The house, called Acorn, is run by a charity and is 100 metres from Oak, the 'first night' centre. Its entrance walls were once covered with the names of children who lived there, written on paper oak leaves. Applications from mothers-to-be are approved if in the best interests of the child and not detrimental to others. Teenage motherhood is not uncommon but not all mothers are young. Mothers retain parental responsibility and for one client this meant: 'This is the first opportunity I've had to bond with a baby.' Not everyone is so lucky. Some lose their babies naturally or terminate their pregnancies while inside. Others are unsuccessful and have the heartbreak of being turned down by the 'Baby Board' while still pregnant with the baby from whom they will be separated.

The children are not prisoners, and volunteers take babies out in push-chairs to experience life outside the prison. Few stay with their mother beyond 18 months, although each case is assessed individually, and 'separation plans' are made if the child will reach that age during the woman's sentence. CIAO has never had to coach a woman in that situation, yet my first contact with Styal stemmed from when I worked for a charity called After Adoption. My role was raising funds to provide support for parents whose children were taken from them, for those who were adopted, and for the parents who adopted them. This is why a coach saying this many years later meant so much to me:

> At our first session, I met a tearful P who could think of nothing to value about herself, or her life, apart from the baby she was carrying. By the time we said our goodbyes, she had come off antidepressants

and secured herself a job (on the outside) to start once her baby was six months old. She also changed from being unable to understand why her partner wanted to be with her into a young woman who was looking forward, with confidence, to building a close and loving family, with him, for their baby. Her confidence will give that baby a much better chance [of] breaking the cycle of low self-esteem. It will create an environment that will enable that baby to thrive.

For better or for worse?

Women's realization of their ability and need for loving, supportive relationships, and that they deserve them, is very common. At least half of my clients have wanted either to strengthen or to break off their relationships. Some are in prison because of low self-esteem: not saying no to a man, helping support his drug use, starting using drugs through a man, and so on. Coercion, manipulation or bullying by an abusive partner are common, but being able to break off the relationship is not always simple, not least because of needing somewhere else to live if you do.

Vicky's Star had 10s for everything except a 5 for motivation and 3 for relationships on the outside, because of her controlling partner: 'I've never been allowed friends since I've been with him.' She was stuck and we talked about what she wanted instead. After a week she said: 'I've noticed a difference in how I think already. It's more positive. You've made me realize that actually I do know what I want. I know my own mind. I know what I want and I'm in control of my own mind.' She pictured a new reality for herself:

I am at home with the girls [here she had put 'but not with him' but crossed that out to make it positive]. He and I are in touch as amicable friends: catching up occasionally. He sees the kids at weekends and holidays and I'll manage the transition... I have my own social life and I'm happier with the kids doing activities they like doing: swimming and going to the park.

Her own social life meant family dropping round and 'having a laugh, talking, dressing up and going out in town' with a few good friends from the past, from the gym and from going out with her sister. While being coached Vicky left her partner and then believed: 'my life is in my own hands, I have all the answers and can live my life how I want it to be... for myself and for my three children'. For her not being with him any more meant: 'I'll be free. It's just been about him for 11 years. Not being controlled by him means my brain will be relaxed. I'll focus on myself and fulfil my potential.' Her new-found confidence included learning about religion, law and injustice as well as talking, realistically, of doing a degree in future. When we had our final session all her scores were 10s and she said: 'I feel like a completely different person and it's completely down to my life coaching.' In a letter she wrote to the governor she said her coaching 'really helped me in a short space of time' and 'I have realized that I have control of my life.'

Another coach's client said:

> I felt like I was in prison all those years but it is only since we've been discussing it that I saw the parallel with being in here – only he never wore keys. It hit me like a thunderbolt, sat here in Styal prison, when I think what it was like with my husband, the only difference is there wasn't a fence around me.

While 'I'll never let a man rule my life again' is a frequent statement, and having the confidence to move away from men who are not good for them may be common, some women have used coaching to strengthen their relationships. One had a discussion with her partner about her fears about his infidelity while she was inside. When her coach asked 'How do you know he loves you?' she said 'I don't know' – only to turn up at her next session with a side of A4 saying: 'There was loads once I started. I was on a roll.'

Fathers and mothers

Parents can cause a similar confusion of emotions. Someone else's client 'didn't mind coming into prison, as she was glad to get away from family struggles and her dad who wanted to control her life. She was scared of going back out'. This negative dynamic is not uncommon. Another client told me: 'I'm stuck in the middle with my dad. It's about assertiveness. I feel I'm being used and he plays head games with me. He knows how to get information out of me.' She was keen to stop being manipulated about everyone else in her family: 'I want to have that conversation with him. He's asking the wrong person. I'm in here.' As soon as she heard herself say this she grinned and said she was going to call him. She took away the idea of explaining: 'When you do X it makes me feel Y', and when I saw her next she had written out a script and 'role-played' it with a friend until ready to make the call. Her expression and tone told me a real shift on her side of the relationship was underway just as a result of thinking aloud.

A shift in assertiveness has had a huge impact on women's thoughts and actions:

> It's given me the tools to speak up for myself, to say what I really want... I know I can achieve so much more, but I felt for a lot of my life that... I wasn't worthy of doing anything more, so I didn't.

As well as thinking of others, clients have looked at how they can't look after anyone else without looking after themselves, so this is not a purely selfish approach: 'She learnt to put herself in the foreground of her life not the background.' Another coach's client said, 'I wanted my mum and family to think: 'I'm doing fine, yeah. It's good here.' But obviously it's not.' As a result of coaching she wrote to her family to explain how she really was and later said: 'I am now more of my authentic self (not just putting a face on)...Before I met [her coach], it was all inside. Now it is unearthed. My relationship with my mum will be lovely.'

Friends and foe

Prisoners are constantly coming and going. Over 9,000 women were received into custody in 2013 in England with almost 4,000 inside at any one time. That difference of 5,000 reflects the system's turnover or 'churn', and the alternative meanings of that word of upset, seethe or produce mechanically are very apt. Women make up just under 1 in 20 of the overall prison population but 2 in 20 of 'receptions' due to their shorter sentences. Styal may have half the places of HMP Manchester (aka Strangeways), yet a similar number of prisoners passes through both their gates each year. The average stay in Styal is just seven weeks and it is not uncommon for women to be back inside within weeks, not months, of being released. You do not need to be a social scientist to imagine the group dynamics and personal impact of that constant change.

Friendships can be more intense when women are cut off from other networks and support. Surrogate parenting can happen when they are separated from their children. Friendships can break down and be broken when women are moved or released. Some stay separate: 'It's difficult to trust. You're on your own really.' Sexual fluidity, shifting sexual relationships and accusations of sexual assault between prisoners add another dynamic layer for some. A few of my clients have said they are less certain of their sexual orientation after time in Styal when completing our demographic forms, though none have explored that as an issue with me.

There is anger, aggression and exclusion. I have heard little of negative networks and bullying but they do exist and coaching has helped clients deal with them: 'It helped me express feelings without feeling like I'm offending people...In the past I would have dwelt on a problem and let it fester...now I don't take notice of bullies any more.' Another was 'having to be very politically astute inside in order to keep her nose clean'. One woman asked to stay on the wing where she could keep herself to herself, in an attempt to avoid irrefutable allegations of theft or other misdemeanours that might stop her getting parole. A client of mine said some women do not get on with other women at all: 'Men will punch each other and then shake hands and it's over. Women don't let go and it goes on for weeks.' This made it all the more significant when a woman who used to be aggressive told me about a recent incident: 'She said sorry and I accepted it and we hugged one another. Case closed.'

Assertiveness has been a regular issue: 'I'm easily bullied out of my tea and coffee supplies because I can't say no to people.' Coaching has led to breakthroughs in confidence for many: 'I've realized that people didn't need or want anything from me. I used to buy people. I've got used to that word: 'no'. Now I explain that I work for my money'; 'I now have the ability and confidence and the courage to stick to what's best for me and not just to please everyone else'; and 'I think I've sussed it. I just said "No, you can't!"'

Clients have successfully tried being curious about other people's behaviour and one said: 'I wrote down angry feelings instead of getting into loads of trouble. I've found I can express myself (be true to myself) but not hurt others in the process.' A client of mine was not sure what exactly helped her but: 'Officers have said I've calmed down. I don't kick off the way I might have before. It's got to be linked to this: nothing's ever stopped me before. I can't remember my last Red Ticket.'

I am no fan of the 'golden rule'. I do not think you should treat others as you want to be treated. If you want to upset me then buy me a present. I prefer George Bernard Shaw's 'platinum rule': treat others as they want to be treated. It is not as easy, but so much better. One client went so far as to reverse the 'golden rule' and said: 'I do to them what they do to me.' Without thinking I said: 'It actually gives power away to others. They are almost choosing, and certainly influencing, your actions.' She appreciated my point at the same time as I kicked myself for stumbling across the line into judging and advising.

Someone else's client:

> had some rigid views about what was right and wrong. Her relationships with others were often tense through her expression of her judgements. Through coaching she was able to broaden her perspective to move to seeing things as effective and not effective rather than right or wrong, thereby allowing her to appreciate other ways of doing things. This significantly improved her relationship with her pad-mate and the client could see ways of improving her relationship with her daughter on her release.

She 'recognized how everyone is unique and how best to get what she needs by working with others'. Another's view of relationships shifted from how she wanted people to treat her to the impact of how she treated other people.

However, among all this talk of relationships, the haunting words I will never forget are: 'The best family some of them have got is in Styal.'

6   The problems

As all areas of our lives are interlinked, the mental health and relationships described in the previous chapter affect and are affected by the following tales and descriptions of addiction, looking after yourself, physical health, accommodation and meaningful use of time. There is less obvious raw pain here though, and even a typically honest moment connected with employment led to laughter not tears.

Drugs and alcohol: pigeons and pills

Most of us encounter mental health problems at some point but few things are better designed to create or increase mental illness than prisons. The extent to which someone might already be unwell when they commit a crime, or whether it develops due to being in prison, is hard to untangle. In the community, people can mask their mental health problems with the drink or drugs they take to cope, leading to 'dual diagnosis' – i.e. having both mental health and substance misuse problems. So, sometimes it is only when women get to prison that you can see how ill they really are.

Alcohol dependence affects 2 per cent of women in England yet 40 per cent reported having problems on arrival at Styal. Many also admit a drug problem, in spite of being likely to hide or underplay substance misuse for fear of losing their children. Substances are used by many as a safety net or to block things out by 'self-medicating' away memories of abuse and other sources of trauma and unhappiness. Boredom can be another trigger. The impact is not just on women's minds and bodies though, as their offences are often linked to selling or paying for drugs, drunken fighting, driving and so on.

Prison is a chance for some to get clean and recover, which coaching can help support and reinforce: 'If I hadn't come to prison I would've been dead the way I was carrying on.' Clients can look at the underlying problems, benefits and downsides, how far behaviour fits with their values and saying no. There are also many courses and designated 'drug-free' houses in Styal that women can live in, where they may be less likely to be tempted.

Substance misuse is one of the hardest areas to deal with because of the physiological ups and downs of clients who are using drugs, or are even under the influence during sessions. It affects whether they are both well and willing, yet CIAO has taken clients on regardless and it has worked for many, if not all. Both coach and client may have to cope with and learn from relapses, but this is similar in all areas of life where we build new routines and patterns. One client knew the magnitude of the challenge and chose to tackle it in phases; sorting out her alcohol problems immediately, while waiting until the days got lighter before coming off methadone.

Both prescription and street drugs have currency within the prison, with perhaps one in three using them. Both can also be stolen as well as sold. Medication has its upside when clients have their 'meds' in time to be as clear headed as possible for their coaching sessions. The improvements clients have made to their lives can affect their 'meds' or 'script' (prescription) too: 'She had the strength to turn down anti-depressants when healthcare staff wanted to prescribe them for her.'

Stopping drugs from getting into prisons is nigh on impossible and alcohol is readily made from scratch, hence 'hooch mooching' in some prisons where officers search out illegally fermented 'hooch', particularly around Christmas. As well as the traditional mobile delivery system of a human body, there are elaborate ways of getting banned items over prison walls and fences, such as stuffed pigeons and catapults. Released prisoners returning for a new sentence and those let out for any reason will all be under duress to bring back 'orders'. Visitors and anyone else caught smuggling face years inside while, if they make it through security, known users suspected of concealing drugs can have them forced out by other prisoners.

A client of mine moved her drug score down from 10 to 1, acknowledging she had not been telling the truth to me or herself. In retrospect, having to work quite so hard to engage her should have been a bit of a clue, but I have learnt a lot since then. Others' clients had a similar realization and moved on from there: 'She was angry with me and angry with the whole system at the start and then a drug and alcohol programme totally opened her eyes to her denial and other people's.'

Everything does not always go according to plan. A client role-playing a scenario for after release actually agreed to take the 'drugs' the coach was 'pushing' when asked, 'What if you were offered them?' saying, 'I'd take them.' Fortunately, by the time all their sessions were over the coach felt able to tell her: 'You have learnt to be assertive and say "no" to bad relationships and to drugs. You now say that you are 98 per cent able to resist going back to drugs, even when there are "down times".'

The following is a familiar refrain in prisons, but independent follow-up means we know this is definitely true for some of our clients who have left Styal: 'Everything in my life will be different; yeah, everything. As I said before once drugs and alcohol have disappeared I can just put my life back on track and do the things that I've always wanted to do.' Clients have seen different types of addiction too and one:

> effectively considered coaching to be a next stage in her recovery from previous approaches: AA groups had helped but she felt that she had in turn become dependent on them, and coaching had 'liberated' her from that: 'I am no longer an addict.'

Self-care: keeping up appearances

While not all prisoners look after themselves well, the care most women in Styal take over their appearance is far greater than mine. This can be a positive boost as women often score themselves 10 and it is the second area they come to if going clockwise around the Star. Not all clients are up there though and one said: 'I really let myself down. I was really lazy as well. It's time to take care of responsibilities…To stop feeling sorry for myself.' Conversely a client with obsessive compulsive disorder (OCD) wanted 'to get it down to a 6 or 7' as, for her, a 10 was not a good thing: nine months later it stayed at 10, but she said it was 'a 10 for the right reasons now'.

Women predominantly wear their own clothes, although these might be ill fitting if they were given the clothing by the prison or changed weight once inside. Some wear a work uniform for the area where they are employed: tunics or overalls, etc. Women also clean their own clothes, so there is always washing everywhere.

Looking after your appearance is a lot harder in a prison with limited access to showers and baths. There are no glass mirrors that could be smashed and the shards used as blades, and you do not have your own scissors or tweezers and other things it is easy to take for granted. This is one reason you can save up your money for haircuts and beauty treatments from prisoners who are being trained in the salon so they can get a job when they are released.

All this self-care is a far cry from the situation removed from the updated prison rules in 1999. Deleted references in the 1964 version were to 'special accommodation'. This allowed unconvicted prisoners to pay for specially fitted cells complete with private furniture, utensils and a valet – just in case Bertie Wooster ever found himself inside, after Jeeves failed to prevent his imprisonment.

Money: the cost of imprisonment

'Poverty is the mother of crime.' Roman Emperor Marcus Aurelius saw the link between a lack of money and committing crime: it is no coincidence that a greater number of people in prison lived in poverty in the community. Many things have not changed much over the centuries. Most women in the criminal justice system have committed theft or similar crimes, and many are in long-term debt that is sometimes linked to partners' gambling or drug use, as well as women's own actions. The stress of debt can lead to drinking to calm the nerves or dull the pain, yet alcohol often leads to offending, and so it goes on.

The scarcity theory, that being short of something can also make us poor at managing it, makes perfect sense. It is too easy to judge others when you have enough of something yourself. While I may be good at managing money, I became very poor at managing my time when I became exhausted and overwhelmed as CIAO grew. The reason I was able to start coaching in Styal in the first place was because I had run my consultancy business as a social enterprise, focused on creating change not profit. I only paid myself a small salary, gave some of the profit to charities, and kept some in the bank for a rainy day or a global recession. However, while this initially meant I had the time and freedom to do exactly what I wanted, CIAO swiftly grew to become far bigger than me. So, how others cope with scarcity is not for me to judge.

The pound seems to have its own exchange rate in prison and little things can mean so much more. 'Luxuries', as basic as shower gel and branded toothpaste you like the taste of, must be bought at higher prices on far lower wages. If an average weekly wage of £9 is your only income you may need to decide between phone credit, stationery or tobacco to keep you sane. 'Privileges' for good behaviour vary in each prison, but they include the chance of better-paid jobs, more visits and being allowed to spend more of your own money that you have earned or had sent in. The maximum a sentenced prisoner can spend varies depending on the 'level' of privileges they are on: in 2014 this was between £25.50 and £10 a week. Calls to a mobile cost 20p a minute and landlines half that. It might take you two hours to earn enough to buy a single stamp costing over 50p to send a visiting order to your family or friends. The same amount buys you half a bottle of shampoo to clean your hair for those visits. The choices are yours.

Compound interest is something you have less control over. If you enter prison owing your mother, a loan shark and a payday loan company £600, then that swiftly becomes £1,000 and you end up with little to lose. You may then be released with the clothes you arrived in and a £46 discharge grant that has not increased since 1997. That £600 debt has also probably doubled by now. There will be a delay as your benefits payment is processed and, while some may be eligible for money to help secure accommodation on release, that is unlikely to be furnished or even have a fridge. It is hard to make a real fresh start and stay clean in all senses with the mind-wrecking worry of debt hanging over you. As a client said: 'What's the point of looking at bills or what you owe?' Debts make it difficult to get housing and benefits on release too, with all the implications for staying away from crime and being reunited with your children.

There are additional financial penalties for those with convictions. About a third of prisoners have never had a bank account and face problems opening one on release. It can be harder to get insurance and, while I laughed when a member of staff described her huge car insurance quote and a client said, 'It's because you're working with the likes of us', he may have had a point. Insurance problems can have knock-on effects for ex-offenders' mortgages and employment too.

My clients have given me hope though. Caroline was a young woman who wanted to be free of debt and estimated she owed about £8,000. £1,800 to the council, £1,000 of 'bits and pieces' and a £5,000 credit card bill that began as a loan of £1,000. Once she decided this would be one of her goals she devised a strategy find out what she owed and propose payment plans to address the large problems. She was going to take small amounts of cash out of the Post Office: '£20 at a time or £30 at the most' and write a shopping list for food and other things that she would stick to. She also knew she would save £30 a month not buying hair things, air fresheners, make-up and cigarettes. As fiscal plans go I do not think a Citizens Advice Bureau volunteer could improve much on that.

It is not just a lack of money that can be the problem but social interaction and innumeracy. Wanting to avoid conversations meant a professional client ordered clothes from catalogues. In a similar vein, another very bright CIAO client stole and travelled on trains without tickets because she was embarrassed at strangers realizing she was financially illiterate and could not cope with looking stupid when unable to add things up and work out the right change. This pride meant she had never explained this to anyone before and, sadly, had no intention of admitting it to anyone else who could help her now.

Physical health: a chance to be well

Each woman in the queue for healthcare is one of 85,000 appointments with a doctor, nurse or other professional every year in Styal alone, or waiting for one of the 240,000 distributions of medication. That is 185 appointments per woman each year or one every other day. Much as these 2010 figures may have changed since we began in Styal you can be sure they will still be staggering.

If I learnt anything in my time as a consultant for the Department of Health and the Ministry of Justice, it is that healthcare is not about creating stronger, fitter criminals, but about dealing with the complex needs of people who are often some of the most socially excluded and deprived in our society. Prisoners are screened for mental and physical health problems when they arrive as it is a real chance to improve health so that they can work, sort their lives out and address other things that prevent them going straight. Prisons do not have hospitals, so women are escorted there with an appropriate number of officers when it is essential. Many years ago I ran a student organization called 'Support for the Homeless' and someone was surprised at why sport was a priority. I have learnt to pronounce 'support' more clearly since then, but exercise matters in prison as much as anywhere. So does the good night's sleep that can be equally elusive.

I need to eat a lot but have never eaten food from the central kitchen nor at the self-catering houses. I have only eaten at the staff bistro, where prisoners have the opportunity to develop and practise both catering and service skills. The daily cost of all the food provided for a prisoner is under £2 so I would not have the luxury of the three breakfasts I need to keep my ridiculous body from rattling and working well. I could order more food from the set list of the prison supplier, known as 'canteen', and a client worked out she could grow herbs, but many things remain unobtainable. This is particularly obvious on hot, sunny days when an ice-cream van's jingle carries through the still air from the other world beyond the fence.

Weight loss is as common a theme inside as it is outside. One client had such a disabling problem that she could not walk. She worked with her coach to take 'baby steps', as she put it, and build up until she could cope and work in prison. Prison staff confirmed she 'changed drastically… grew in confidence' and became a 'self-starter'. Within weeks she became a lot more independent: 'I've lost a lot of weight… and I've learned to walk as well, even though it hurts.' Physical changes and mental shifts so often go hand in hand. Women can be very underweight too, particularly those with a history of drug misuse. My client who struggled with this said: 'I wanna be eatin. I don't eat but I don't wanna die.'

Women walking around with their own mugs, like office workers' paper coffee cups, are a reminder of the high prevalence of diseases such as hepatitis. This has led coaches to weigh up our humanity against possible risks to our health. One coach was clear about this: 'What felt best? When both clients made me a coffee from their own coffee supply and showed genuine rapport with me – I got a hug.' Tea and coffee are a currency of sorts, so a client offering a coach a drink from their limited supply was a far greater gift than from a professional client and as near as you could get to payment. Not to take it was unthinkable and totally worth the risk for her.

When I told a governor I had been mistaken for a prisoner yet again he asked me to smile and said: 'Nah, your teeth are too good!' The dentist is kept busy in Styal and the bad teeth that result from drug abuse can stop people smiling, hold them back in applying for jobs, and so on. Sorting these out while being coached has a huge impact:

> I have watched her confidence grow and grow. It has been especially rewarding to see her change physically (she has new teeth) and to discuss the effect that this has had on her. She has been amazed at how far she has come in so little time.

Nearly four times as many women prisoners smoke as in the community, so money for tobacco is important. Our clients have been ingenious and bloody-minded in their responses to this. One stopped smoking:

> Nine months ago and although she has put on weight she looks so much better for it. She said that she did it as soon as people stopped nagging her about stopping. She had smoked for 50 years. She used patches for a few days but then didn't need any help.

The client with the eating problem tied her solution in with a friend's smoking: 'So I would eat I made a bet wiv someone that if they stopped smoking I'd eat and they have 'n' I have started eating.'

While all prisoners should be able to spend half an hour to an hour in the open air each day, things such as walking where and when you want are not an option. There is a gym like a traditional school assembly hall, with a stage and offices at the front and a sports field behind. Understandable limitations restrict activities such as the Duke of Edinburgh Awards but staff do all they can with these and other courses. One thing you never do in a prison is run, unless you are in the gym. Running happens when all is not well and urgent assistance is required from officers. You do not want to be known as the person who caused a stampede, however late you may be for your coaching session. Instead, the gym's stage is home to modern treadmills, where you can run without causing alarm. Do not think this is a luxury health spa though. When I asked Rebecca what she really enjoyed when she was 6 years old she said 'swimming' and we both sighed. Yet another reminder of why it is best not to ask a client to look back when they are stuck inside. There are also cycling machines, which echo the old treadwheels that once turned grain into flour for prisoners' bread elsewhere. Wasting pedalling energy going nowhere is nightmarish for me. I am never more aware of the freedom my bike gives than when I am cycling to Styal, collecting my thoughts as I push up the small, steep hills beforehand. I would miss that bedrock of my physical and mental health more than almost anything.

Accommodation: a room of your own?

While you may not have to pay rent, even a client with a positive view of Styal said:

> It's a good place to live but you don't have the freedom. You get the food and you get the bed but you get shouted at and you have to do what others want. It's gorgeous out there and we're locked in here.

At this point it did cross my mind that I was locked in of my own free will on a glorious Saturday morning. The reminders that you are in prison are audible too. Clients never flicker in response to the siren indicating when women are allowed to move around freely, whereas I still flinch filled with low dread, just as when professionals ignore the screech of a practice fire alarm while the coach looks for signs of panic.

For some, prison can be a cocoon or a relief and release from the world outside: 'Coming to prison is the best thing that's ever happened to me.' For others it is hell on earth. I have seen a flooded cell but never had to face the stomach-turning euphemism of a 'dirty protest' with the occupant's excrement or food smeared on the walls and sometimes thrown at staff. When you are 'banged up' is when you are locked in with your own thoughts or you might be 'padded up' in one of Styal's shared cells or small dormitories. Some are allowed their own personal furnishings such as duvets, cushions, rugs and plants, but no one has satellite TV. One of the things that surprised me most was the appearance of a sign asking anyone entering a house to keep the door shut so the cat did not get out. An officer had brought her in and prisoners paid for all her food and other needs. The animal's presence brought a greater sense of humanity to the unit and was particularly joyful for me, as I would miss our black rescue cats terribly if I were inside.

Prisoners can mix, so someone who has been sentenced for shoplifting razor blades can be in a cell next door to a woman in for murder, though who shares with whom aims to take into account women's needs for companionship and their vulnerability. Once, when showing new coaches around, we talked to three women in their shared room who were welcoming a new prisoner. She looked terrified of the noisy world she had entered and when names were shouted out by the officer downstairs they all jumped to attention. Bullying is reported as low in Styal, where women generally feel quite safe, though one said: 'There is so much fear inside. Women are scared to let it out and show weakness.'

The human aspect of coaching can make it all too easy to forget we are working in a prison, yet simple actions such as going up to clients' rooms without a house officer knowing can put us at risk of being taken hostage, groomed, manipulated and accused of passing drugs, among other things. On one occasion when a coach went upstairs she was very firmly but politely reminded that those dormitories were in fact cells.

I may be gregarious, and was able to share a dormitory with 20 girls at school, but I value my space and freedom now and need my solitude too. There was once a policy of strict silence in prisons but they are noisy places these days and it is hard to find peace. The impact of everything is greater inside, where you cannot always just walk away from people if you have an argument nor seek the comfort and support of those you love.

All humanity is in Styal and I have heard how pad-mates 'stink', are 'messy', have mental health problems, self-harm, are withdrawing from drugs and so on. The majority have a hotel-type safe and a personal 'privy' key to their dorm or cell if it is shared, but personal belongings can still go missing. If you are in a dorm with other prisoners you have to come up with different strategies for dealing with problems. My client who said 'I use a quilt to cover my head. I don't want to hurt anyone so I try to prevent myself doing it' changed this by the next session to 'Now I don't even want to do it' as she had worked out how to let things go. A client of mine who also struggled with the chaos around her realized she could not control everything and said:

> Now I notice things aren't how I'd like them to be (like someone spilling an ashtray on the floor or disrespecting an officer) but they don't bother me. People and officers can look after themselves. I'm less judgemental... It's their opinions.

A client who struggled with not having her own space came up with the idea of music, exercise, dreaming, sleeping and reading a book as ways she might escape from the prison. After discounting the first two, as they did not fit her situation, we took the third further and I asked where she would rather be. She pictured herself by the sea in summer watching the waves with the smell of fresh doughnuts and taste of the candyfloss and ice cream, as she listened to the noise of the crowds in the arcades, the shrieks of the gulls and the rumble of the roller-coaster. She could conjure up this other world whenever she wanted by holding a seashell (or more prosaic equivalent) to her ear and it meant she could now relax: 'when I want my space'.

This search for space once someone is released is a common challenge too. Housing is radical in the sense that it gives us the roots we need to put down to settle. I have been homeless for a very brief time, so have the tiniest sense of just how unsettling it can be. Humans need to be in the right place to move forward – mentally and physically – with a secure base of both who we are and where we are. More women than men can lose their home because they are much more likely to be the sole adult. Having a suitable home is also linked to getting your children back or, at least, having them to visit – the circular catch being that getting housing is more likely if your children are already living with you. Finding somewhere where you will not be surrounded by drugs or alcohol when trying to stay clean adds to the difficulty. If you are homeless before being sent to prison you are more likely to be reconvicted on release. Even if you have accommodation arranged, being in a hostel or sleeping on a friend's sofa is not ideal. However, poor or non-existent credit ratings also make guaranteeing rent hard. Finding housing of their own has been a goal for a few of my clients.

Maureen pictured a calm, peaceful two-bedroom house to which she returned from work and her daughter returned from school to do her homework so she could achieve her dream of becoming a police officer. It was white and clean, with a Japanese Akita dog living there with them. She mapped out the financial cost of this in detail, including travelling to work, and set about doing all she could to find a job and start the process of finding accommodation while she was still inside. Saving money and giving this to her mum was an important part of this goal for her as well.

There are numerous reasons for sleepless nights. I have never spent a night inside and it must be a different world. Many go to bed early but this is not always a release: 'I only get three hours sleep a night. I just can't relax and think straight.' The impact of good sleep on both recovery from mental health problems and in creating them is huge. As Styal was once an old orphanage, some women also tell of hearing children crying and even sensing their physical presence. 'Every single one of us cries, sometimes every night', and they will be crying into a pillow in which many other prisoners have buried their faces.

Meaningful use of time: this is your life

The first jail I ever went into was Pentonville, and it struck me that prisons waste time. Everyone's time. Then, when we began coaching in Styal, clients told their coaches things like: 'I was sent to prison for a reason. I have had the luxury of being in here and have had the time to think about what I've done and what I will do in the future' and 'I wish I could stay a bit longer so I could do a bit more.'

Einstein would love the parallel universe of 'prison time'. Prisons have a zone all of their own, with mealtimes to fit the system and prompt attendance at appointments being an *Alice in Wonderland* dream. The perception of time shifts too, particularly for those in 'for a while': warped and twisted with endless repetition. At least lifers are in prison though. It is chilling to think some of our clients would have been executed in this country in the past, or in other countries now. However, none of this diminishes the unimaginable and unending pain for victims and their families.

Prisoners should spend a minimum of 12 hours out of their cells every day (subject to security, control and discipline) and 42 hours of each week in structured activities. They are also required to work and can be ordered to do so, but the prison cannot make women do anything. If a lawful order is disobeyed a prisoner can be 'charged' and judged by a manager at an 'adjudication'. Punishments include fines or losing privileges (such as the right to visits or association or to buy additional food or toiletries) or even having more days added on to a sentence. So, in theory, refusing to comply might lead to being locked up with no TV and just four walls for company. The aim is to make life as normal as possible through a working routine. The reality is that the 'regime', the work and sheer exhaustion of being in prison, can mean there is much less time and energy for coaching than you might imagine. The structure is a boon to many, as two of my clients said: 'You can't be any more secure than here. It's a comfort blanket: the structured life and routine.' and 'Some people in here don't want to choose. That's why people get stuck in the system, 'cos it's easier isn't it? No choice. For instance they don't like being unlocked at lunchtime. All they've got is their routine.'

Life is not just about time though, but about meaning. It is not just about the near-constant mopping and polishing of floors seen in every prison I have ever been in. If we can make our lives meaningful they can become bearable. My client who said drinking was 'just something to do' began to look for other things to do when she was released and set a goal just to drink at the weekends, not every day. Someone else's client found something she really wanted to do and work on because in the past 'I've never woken up and thought what a lovely day. Now I feel it's worth getting up in the morning.'

Education past and present

Coaching as a learning process is one of the purest forms of education in the word's literal sense of leading and drawing out the client's own thinking and answers. As one client said: 'I never had the chance to go to university, thanks to this process I feel as if I've got as much out of this as had I done that.' I know it is my educational privilege that has enabled me to set up CIAO but, until I mentioned David Cameron and a client asked who he was, I did not realize just how different frames of reference can be.

About a third of women in prison truanted, were permanently excluded or left school before they were 16. Two-thirds have no qualifications whatsoever. We were all alert to low literacy and numeracy, knowing many prisoners have to ask someone else to read and write letters to their partner or others. However, all my clients have been literate and we remain keen to work with those who are not. At least we know Coaching Champions recruiting by word of mouth means we are not solely reliant on women being able to read our posters. Radio means we can reach all prisoners too, however long they are inside, so early on clients and I were interviewed in the Prison Radio Association's studio for the prison's own station. Styalistic Radio can be heard through TVs across Styal and feeds into and receives radio features from National Prison Radio. Clients have done the radio production course as well.

None of the educational statistics tell you whether or not women in prison are bright though. I have lost track of how many clients no longer think they are lazy or stupid now that they have been coached. Stopping going to school at 12, often as a result of 'trouble' at home, is not an accurate indicator of intelligence. Another coach reflected on 'the time I spend working with people who already have had plenty of development and privilege compared to [my client] and how adult and motivated she has been compared to some of them!'

Most prisoners have access to courses and training, as employment makes them much less likely to commit crime. Education is provided by The Manchester College, not the prison itself. Vocational training means women can gain qualifications like City & Guilds, in fields such as painting and decorating, industrial cleaning and catering. Clients have trained to be a plumber, qualified as a librarian and explored an embalming course (for which research proved a challenge, to say nothing of the practical element). Catering was easier: 'I've learnt more here in seven months in the kitchen making stuff from scratch, not just from frozen, than I have on the out in a canteen.' Not all learning takes places in classrooms either, nor is it the 'College of Crime' some imagine. A client of mine asked prisoners from Romania to help her learn Romanian in order to be able to speak with them. I love that higher education is possible through the Open University with whose Business School I have studied over the years too. It is also apt that this book is published by Open University Press. One of our clients achieved a distinction for her Open University humanities course and biography writing course. She wrote a script for the Christmas play and started a group for other prisoners because writing helped her sort out her emotions and she hoped it would do the same for others.

'I can't get a job. My family will disown me'

People rarely accuse a family of lawyers or doctors of a 'poverty of imagination'. Many choose careers because of familiarity and unspoken expectation. Yet there can be a very different pressure in prison. As a client said: 'I can't get a job. My family will disown me.' Far from all prisoners come from such backgrounds though. Members of my family have served time and I have worked with the Partners of Prisoners and Families Support Group (POPS) through whom I heard a mother say of reporting her son to the police: 'it was hard getting him arrested'.

Styal can help women who want to move on in many ways. Employment is available in most areas of the prison to enable it to run smoothly. These include the gym, health centre and library. Styal also has the first of The Clink Charity restaurants to be set up in a women's prison. This expanding chain trains prisoners to cook and do front of house, before finding them employment on release.

The gardens and polytunnels yield flowers and vegetables you can buy through an honesty box. You used to be able to hear the sound of bees in the prison's hives as well, though they are empty at the moment. Many of the 50 or so women contribute to and benefit from working day to day with the peace and smell of moist, warm earth. They also regularly win awards at the Royal Horticultural Show in nearby Tatton Park. One year the theme was 'metamorphosis' with a transformation from a dark cell to light. Some members of the public were similarly changed when they realized the knowledgeable women talking about the scheme's plants were prisoners on day release.

I coached Suzanne about finding employment while sitting in a half-glazed box at one end of the wing. The windows meant the coaching was accompanied by a series of friendly knocks and faces saying hello until I told them to go away in a slightly unorthodox fashion, which led to much laughter and peace at last. Suzanne gave herself a 4 for motivation at the start. The second time we met she had booked appointments with other services inside and looked at both benefits and work opportunities, as well as how to describe the gap on her CV and how and when to disclose her criminal conviction. She swiftly came up with job search ideas that excited her about the possibilities, rather than being despondent, and felt coaching 'put things in order'.

Once Suzanne was out she would face a tough market-place, though clients who have never worked before have left with NVQs and a job lined up. One's coach said: 'She was scared about facing the world after a year behind bars. "What will it be like? Will they accept me? Will I be good enough?"' The coach then used GROW to help her feel more confident about supporting herself going to her job on the first day and explored how challenges she had faced and overcome inside might help her outside. 'It was quite delightful how energetic she was.'

While one in five employers say they do or may exclude someone with a criminal record from being recruited, a few enlightened organizations actively recruit from prisons – such as Timpson the cobblers. Timpson has full-time training facilities in a number of prisons, though not Styal, and is proud of how its hand-picked 'colleagues' contribute to the profitability of the business, including some who 'work out'. In prison 'working out' means being released on temporary licence (ROTL'd) to work or train in the community towards the end of your sentence, not going to the gym. This can happen if you are not thought a risk to the public nor likely to commit further crime. Women who are ROTL'd often return exhausted at the end of each day.

Many women in Styal have criminal records of an indelible kind, whether scars, inflicted by themselves or others, or prison tattoos. A client who wanted an active and exhausting job hated the Job Centre and did not apply for jobs because she felt the scars where she had cut herself elicited judgement. This echoes a client who said that before coaching she felt 'impregnated with shame, like a tattoo'. Thanks to coaching, some clients are now better placed to interact and secure a job:

> I'm now able to participate in groups and I can speak in front of people. I'm not shy and I would say it's through doing the coaching. I think that my life will be a lot different in a good way because I feel I've got the confidence to go to job interviews and just the confidence to talk to people, which was a big issue.

'Shit at shoplifting'

Many years ago the governor of Strangeways told me that men in his prison were generally not risk averse. CIAO's clients have proved this to be the case in the best possible ways, including writing business plans and setting up their own businesses inside and out. They can take time to realize their potential though: 'She was extremely upset when I first saw her, then she felt it had all resolved itself magically in between sessions and didn't see herself as an agent of change.' This woman has now explored setting up a business inside the prison.

Others are already entrepreneurial in different ways. The options available to women really hit home when Em talked me through her scores on the Outcomes Star in relation to finances and work. Whenever her children's father was locked up in prison she earned what she needed to support them all by working on the streets, because 'I'm shit at shop-lifting.' The two of us burst out laughing only to reflect on how she had thought carefully about her career options, weighed up where her skills lay and pursued a logical path. Exactly like my professional clients in some ways, and yet so very different in the choices she felt she had. After coaching, Em's sights were set on college and less dangerous forms of employment that extended beyond prostitution and theft.

This reminded me of my first contract as a consultant when Manchester Action on Street Health (MASH) asked me to design mentoring support for sex workers. Talking about what might work for them I saw a hard side of life and deepened my respect for the courage of women, men, girls and boys who survive on the streets and elsewhere, relying solely on their bodies and their wits. Issues around self-esteem are complex and there are strong links between drug and alcohol use and street-based prostitution, as well as theft. However, whatever your moral position, children still need food and shoes.

Groundhog day

As well as CIAO's clients gaining employment inside the prison, taking up opportunities for training and development and finding jobs after release, many also want to help others and learn coaching skills themselves.

One of our proudest successes is Tess, who was in prison for a long while and said her life was 'like groundhog day'. After coaching she was transformed, saw things in a bigger context and became 'a real planner – memorials, additional courses, moving houses, getting others to do learning, taking courses and planning next steps... 24/7 cover for vulnerable prisoners'. She set about playing a part in prisoners' lives in other ways and in making the prison better for staff too. Now she is looking 'like a woman with a mission' and is the greatest Champion of coaching in Styal.

It's given me so much confidence it's unbelievable. I wouldn't have done half the things I've done now. It's taught me so much. I never thought I would say you could feel independent in prison – but from this experience – I do.

7   Who are you?

'Miss! Miss! Who are you?' is the commonest question I am asked in Styal.
It is also the fundamental one we ask our clients. It is not easy to be true
to yourself and have the courage to be who you really are anywhere, let
alone in prison. This is why values are the second of the three essential
areas coaches explore. This chapter also looks at how my attitude and
appearance work for and against me, how CIAO can only work in the
prison thanks to the support of hundreds of other people and their services, and how we are so careful with prisoners' personal information that
we occasionally forget their names.

Know yourself

Coaching is radical. It gets to the root of who we are and what makes us
human. Coaches want to increase clients' self-awareness, so they understand how they think and interact. Values are fundamental to how we
make decisions and what we say and do. Values are the personal ideals
or core principles which are important to you in your life. They are about
who you are (not who you were, nor who you think you should be) and
what is important to you (not who is important to you).

Articulating values can help a client make decisions and affect their
motivation to change. Being true to your values can then help you be more
content, whereas if you ignore your values, or someone does something
which challenges them, you are likely to feel discomfort or even anger.
Knowing what makes you happy and angry is particularly essential in the
claustrophobia of a prison. Understanding the trigger of someone 'tread-
ing on your values' can be literally vital in helping a client cope and not
lash out. As a client said: values 'make sense of things'. However, because
values are abstract compared to more concrete goals, we often look at

them later, once we have a sense of what they might be. Sometimes a client can be stuck about moving forward or knowing what they want from life at the start of coaching, and looking at values can work then too.

If your actions, goals and values do not align you can feel it, even if that compromise just shows as feeling unsettled, rather than mental distress. This feeling can also arise from a value a client realizes she has inherited or picked up from people she no longer feels in tune with. This realization can prompt her to let go of both the value itself and the negative connections. Looking at the values that serve her well can prompt similar realizations.

Personal values are why you have to be very clever to punish someone effectively (for example, I was always happy to be sent to my room as a child). The law is not bespoke enough to take away what is most valuable to each individual, nor is it instant and unavoidable. It really breaks down if someone's childhood included promises that were never kept. Why would anyone delay gratification if they never believed their effort or pain would be rewarded?

We help our clients look inside themselves to understand what really matters to them and to increase their awareness of how they see others and vice versa. Coaching can be a mirror: reflecting a client's words or actions so they can consider and reflect on their impact and reactions. Like the surface of a pond, this reflection is clearer with stillness and time. Holding up a mirror can lead to initial preening as a client receives true attention, perhaps for the first time ever. Then, as they focus more, they can recognize and see themselves more accurately.

Changing your behaviour and reaching your goals can be tough. Knowing your values can clarify what you really want and motivate you to keep going as your habits gradually change and others begin to notice. Socrates, one of the most famous prisoners of all time, said 'the unexamined life is not worth living', echoing the ancient Greek instruction above the Temple of Apollo at Delphi that implies we should not just 'know ourselves', but recognize ourselves and our limits too. Socrates would appreciate our approach as he described his own role as a 'midwife of the mind' who helped others find their own answers. This metaphor came close to realization once when I entered the mother and baby unit only to be asked: 'Are you the midwife?' One of my few moments of panic in Styal.

What's been trodden on?

Many of my clients find it useful to work out what values were 'trodden on' when they are angry, frustrated or upset: what the activities, things and people they love give them. What money or 'family' give you (security, status, freedom to do what you want, something else) can help unlock your values too. Uncovering 10 or so words that sum up what is important to you can take time. There is no 'right' or 'wrong' answer. You can play around with them to work out if they really fit you. I prefer to give all my clients a blank sheet of paper, rather than a list of ready-made values that is a 'pick and mix' where you can just like the look of something, rather than think through what is really you. Having said this, scanning a list after the hard work is done can trigger useful missing thoughts.

My early clients' top five values in Styal were: independence, helping others, openness, fairness and respect. I have never had a client with whom I did not have values in common. This may be partly due to priming and who puts themselves forward for coaching. However, I have come across very little greed and seen far more protectiveness, rather than selfishness, in my clients, contrary to what some might expect.

Working out your values can be very moving and an insight into what you lose in prison, as well as how much clients have to give. One client lit up at the possibilities her values showed her and at knowing

> what the keys to my emotions are...honesty, trust, equality, contributing back to the world – doing something constructive, earning – a sense of pride and knowing I've done it, safety – not dealing with lies and accusations of lies, space – able to shut the door and my grown up little girl being able to come to see me, freedom – the buzz of running, and integrity – sticking up for what you believe in.

Before we had our own coaching rooms I was in a building where women met the many agencies who come into Styal to help them get their lives back on track. The clear glass windows made the interview rooms goldfish bowls from the waist up. You could still lose yourselves in the moment though, even when the coach was nearest the door, as security requires. It was here one client worked out her values. When we finally looked down at them written out neatly she said: 'I like the person I am really and I didn't think I did. That's shocked me that has.' As she started crying, I swapped sides of the table so she faced me and the solid outer wall. Humanity overrode security in that moment. No one else needed to see the tears of revelation rolling down her cheeks.

What do you value about yourself?

Styal emphasizes the fact that humans do not function well if worried or scared, let alone scarred. However, many women in prison have far greater untapped potential than most of my professional clients.

Initially we asked, 'What three things do you value about yourself?' at the introductory session, and 'What three things do you value about your life?' Low self-esteem meant clients really struggled with things about themselves, whereas they could come up with things about their lives, which are more about gratitude. We decided to ask them to consider this after the first proper coaching session but then dropped it altogether. One client did come up with: 'despite all the odds I'm still 'ere' but even she said, 'it was 'ard and I didn't like the fact I couldn't think of three things'.

A client who could not accept positive things about herself realized 'it's because I was bullied... I've never said that before'. Another assumed any compliments meant someone was 'taking the mick'. I went further with one of my clients when we dealt with the British affliction of being unable to accept praise. She learnt how to acknowledge and deflect positive comments with the neat trick of simply saying 'thank you'.

Rebecca was struggling to come up with anything more than 'I'm good at cleaning' or, as she put it with a grin, 'I'm a good scrubber!' So I told her I valued her bravery in being the first person to be coached, the honesty of her responses, her courage in daring to set things straight the day after our first session, her beauty and her intelligence. She looked stunned and I was not surprised, when I asked if she wanted to write these things down, that she said no. However, she came up with two things of her own when we next met just days later. She said she was a good listener and helped others. This realization meant she decided to do a mentoring course and volunteer with families of women in prison after she was released. Confessing her strengths to herself had as great an impact as confessing her secrets to her partner, if not greater.

Someone else's client took this to its conclusion:

I found coaching very enlightening. I have been able to see myself more honestly. I have learnt it is okay to be me. I am good enough. I like myself today. I have learnt to let go of the concepts that did not serve me well. I have learnt to recognize how far I have developed and feel proud of myself. I value my stability, relationships, freedom in mind, body and spirit. I value [me].

Uncovering their values has also helped women make sense of their relationships and to plan for future generations: 'Recognizing the VALUES that are important to me has helped me turn things into positives.' This client was undermined by her father from the age of 11, but working out her values helped her move on. She decided to put him 'in a box' where he could not affect her any more, as there were more important things for her to think about in life. Her coach said:

She is more honest about her own feelings now, rather than, when asked, saying that everything is great when it isn't. She can have a little cry and then get on with things, where previously she would have held her true feelings inside and been more stressed because of the effort that took.

Who women are in Styal is also often linked with their children, who can be a great motivating force, not just linked back to their parents. In Rebecca's second session, talking about her children brought tears to her eyes and moved me to put my hand on her arm. The next time we met I asked what she wanted for her children and she imagined looking back with pride at herself and them in 20 years' time. What she wanted was 'to have been a good role model and a good mum – to set boundaries for their own good' and for them to have a good life and children of their own. She also wanted them to be: 'Good people, really polite, well educated (going to university if they want), married or in a stable relationship, and close to each other.' Another example of how so many of our dreams are the same, wherever we are.

Who am I?

Unsurprisingly, my top three values of fairness, growth and independence are at the heart of CIAO's approach. Every last thing that we do is all about fairness. From a very young age we are told 'life is unfair' but I never accepted we should just leave it at that. I believe we should do all we can to make life fairer.

I trained as a coach in 2003 when it dawned on me that not everyone was as interested in the benefit of my great wisdom as I thought and other forms of learning might be better. The solutions I work out to suit my character and circumstances are unlikely to be perfect for you. I learnt the depth of this truth when I coached my husband. I did not know enough to solve the problems of the man I know well and live with, but he was able to work them out through coaching. So why would I try any other approach with women in Styal or others anywhere? This was when I realized coaching is the best way for me to help others grow, and for me to grow and learn myself.

I am happy to risk getting things wrong, very good at actually getting things wrong and quite happy to admit to both. I fall over a lot, literally and metaphorically, and have the scars to prove it. Being vulnerable means, by definition, we are more likely to be hurt, but pushing the limits means we live life to the full.

Being given and taking responsibility has been essential to me from an early age. I was brought up to be independent and to serve others.

Rank means nothing to me in spite of years living all over the world as an RAF child. I struggle in any hierarchical organization – like a prison, for instance. I do not know my place and neither do others. I even struggle in the charity I set up to achieve something I care deeply about. A prison governor once said: 'Now I know you're a fighter pilot's daughter your arrogant, "can do", gung ho, "will win" kind of attitude makes perfect sense.' He added, slightly belatedly, 'I mean arrogant in a good way.'

My independence extends to all of my life. A member of prison staff told me I was lucky having a rich husband who let me do what I do. By some miracle I kept my composure long enough to explain my consultancy earned every penny that enabled me to work for CIAO without payment. I am financially independent and it was entirely my choice to invest years of savings in CIAO and women in Styal. Even now that raises my blood pressure, at the same time as bringing a smile to my face.

The 'Clare Trap'

Do you talk to strangers? I do all the time: in queues, on buses or online. I am curious. I start up unexpected conversations and ask inappropriate questions. I don't suffer embarrassment and am partly fearless, partly oblivious, with an inner belief and supreme confidence. I am comfortable when people are angry or negative, as my gut reaction can be like that too, although I'm slowly becoming better at processing it and acting on feedback afterwards. My personal security means I have little fear of loss or of rejection by strangers. I expect a warm, positive response and for people to say yes. I certainly never thought of our work in Styal as a pilot.

A friend asked how I managed to work with prisoners in Styal. This is a fair question as my previous boss referred to me as 'pink cheeks, posh voice'. I really had to think about it but what follows is part of the answer.

I'm very tactile and liable to give clients exuberant hugs, but shaking hands at the start has felt too formal with almost all of them, so generally I just smile broadly, say hello and settle down. I asked one client why she had felt comfortable with me from our first meeting and she said it was my friendly approach, initial greeting, warmth and eye contact. That made me smile, as one of my professional clients says my coaching is all in 'that look' with my head cocked and eyes slightly narrowed or opened a bit wider according to what I have just heard. Someone else said: 'You're looking frowny' to which I could only say 'I'm sorry. This is my "thinking face".' In my mind I aim for an open 'Tell me more?' face; gently curious and non-judgemental but not blindly agreeing either, whereas another coach told me 'Oh, don't do that face again! Your face is normally so expressive.' I suspect this means on that occasion my attempt at a blank canvas gave the impression someone had stolen my soul.

I look away to think a lot and look down at my notes, as well as gazing at my client. It all depends on what we both need. For those uncomfortable with eye contact I look away more to talk if they glance back, so they can watch me as I speak. I love how conversation flows when you walk with someone in line with Aristotle's peripatetic philosophy but, sadly, have never done a walking and talking session in Styal. I do wonder about how you can tell if someone is telling that truth more accurately from their voice alone. Looking away may even give me a better sense of how much a client believes what they are saying themselves.

Eye contact is always fascinating. A client who had been in Styal for less than a day barely glanced at me at first. After we had been together a while she looked me in the eye, eventually smiled wryly and before I left an hour later was able to laugh, which she had not done in weeks. It was a huge relief to know she was in an infinitely better place than when we met.

To quote from my husband's wedding speech:

> Clare has a remarkably positive outlook on life, with little concept of embarrassment. She lures people into conversations with the Clare Trap. On trains, buses, walking in the street, wherever, the Clare Trap is normally an abstract comment to someone. The normal reticence people have is blown away by the relief when they understand what Clare is saying. With the person now engaged in conversation, the next stage of the Trap then follows as Clare changes the topic to something completely different. By the time this is worked through people feel they are well on the way to a lifelong friendship.

I think it is about being genuinely curious, warm and human. I am very happy sharing my many idiocies so that, as a client said: 'By being very honest and open in your questioning it draws out an honest response in me and makes me be honest with myself.'

Are you for real?

I like simplicity and authenticity. I like things to look as they are. I am very happy in my own skin and dislike veneers or facades, whether on tables, buildings or people. I do not wear a mask of make-up but many other very effective coaches do. I rarely wear my wedding ring on my finger anywhere but always wear it around my neck in the prison and ask clients to call me 'Clare' not the standard 'Miss'. Being myself is not always to everyone's delight though and can be messier for systems. The downside of being true to my strong self-belief and ego the size of a planet is I have never knowingly been described as humble. When prompted to ask my husband 'What's the one the thing I'm not good at?' he said 'Humility?' I had throwing in mind, but am happily used to being mocked.

Exhortations to 'develop your signature presence' make me sigh. Why not just be you? Clients sense if you are for real. I find it helpful and natural to go to where my clients are: matching them mentally and physically in terms of their energy, as well as their posture and position. I am hopeless at sitting up straight, so sit sideways, lean back, or sit on the floor of the wing with my client on a chair alongside with the smell of disinfectant and floor polish all around. This is partly because of my long back and legs but mainly my preference. Humility may not be my style but being grounded is. As one client told someone else about me: 'She's safe. She's sound. She's dead relaxed.' I have sat on a pavement with someone living on the streets before sharing a meal with him and handing over my socks and a fiver. Goodness knows what the rest of the pub thought was going on but we both ended the evening happier than when we met.

We are judged by how we look and sound, whether we like it or not. I am naturally scruffy and have been treated very differently as a visitor by some other prisons, depending on whether I was wearing a suit or jeans. My looks generally work in my favour, however deceptive they might be. One friend said I had a strong line in faux innocence. I do not alter my public school accent, nor do I completely abstain from swearing when working one to one if I sense the person would be comfortable with it. I generally hold back with a group as I would with professional clients, though. I know some people are relieved and delighted when I swear. Perhaps it shows I am not as straight as stereotypes imply and they feel they can relax and be themselves a little more. Apparently my voice can help too: 'You always bring me down from a manic place. I think it's your accent! It's a really calming voice. It's like cotton wool in a way.' The same voice has also had an unintended effect on an exhausted professional client. That was the last time I let a police officer shut their eyes to think in a comfortable chair. I need to work on that fine line between calming and soporific. At least no CIAO client has ever fallen asleep during a session with me.

I am very curious why I am mistaken for a prisoner more than the other coaches. Very few of the coaches share my ridiculously privileged upbringing, so I love the fact that a posh voice doesn't rule me out. I've been taken for a prisoner by prisoners, even when I've had keys on my belt or been asking them a question through an office window. There was even doubt at a probation office once. I do find this disconcerting as I look a little like I'm impersonating a police officer when in Styal, in my 'uniform' of grey jumper, black combats, boots and high-vis cycling jacket. At least they always let me out now.

Who are CIAO?

CIAO's values affected everything we did from the outset. All of us involved in starting CIAO gave what we did without payment because some things really matter in life. This generosity of spirit means at social gatherings coaches overpay and say 'keep the change', rather than quibbling about who had a decaffeinated coffee. From our first proper meeting we agreed we wanted to operate as social enterprise as soon as possible, so we are now paid and valued for the work we do, as well as being able to pay coaches. This way no one is deprived of a living through working for us and we can have as diverse a group of coaches as possible. Nor are we undercutting social businesses who do not benefit from people working without payment. Some coaches may choose to give their payment back if they do not need or want financial reward, others may choose to pay it forward elsewhere. It is entirely up to them.

Articulating our values as a group felt simplistic for such a complex area, though for an external audience and for the completeness of our first social accounts the coaches agreed they were: responsibility, respect and choice. Since then I have been working out CIAO's values the way I would a client's: watching, listening, noting and thinking over time. They are still not written down because if they were made explicit people would have to make sense of them and it's easy to tear the soul out of the very words designed to bring people together.

We want to push ourselves, as well as our clients. We aim to equip people with what they need to know to coach safely, while giving them the freedom to coach in the way they know best. Growth, learning and developing are at our heart and this is supported by capturing and sharing feedback among ourselves, and more widely, so that we can continue to improve. I dream of things being simple and flexible, as we do not want to add bureaucracy but to take it away. The balance of being effective, providing excellent quality and capturing how we are doing all that is constantly shifting, however much I try to be efficient and economical in terms of time, money and the planet. All this has to be fundamentally enjoyable too, as few in CIAO believe we will be rewarded in any afterlife.

We take positive risks around giving our time and energy without any guaranteed return. Even against the odds we have a go and don't stop trying solely because it appears logical to do so. Nobody is beyond forgiveness and we will not write them off, though we may let them move on. We are complex human beings: coaches, staff and clients alike. We have faith and, most importantly, we find others who share that. We are prepared to be surprised that unlikely things happen. However, we don't take risks that might endanger people's lives or personal information. It is literally vital for us to protect coaches, clients and others and to keep them physically and emotionally safe and well.

Other than enthusiasm and friendliness, nothing makes a typical CIAO coach. We are a diverse group in terms of background, culture, race, sexuality, religion and most other respects. I was surprised when people asked whether men could coach, as it never crossed my mind that they should not, and a fifth of our coaches have been male so far. I particularly love the positive circularity of the fact that one of our coaches used to visit his mother in Styal when she was a prisoner there many years ago.

Working with Styal

We work in parallel with the criminal justice system but are not part of it. Life might be easier if we were part of the legitimate process – however, remaining detached and being outside the prison system with no agenda is a critical part of our role. It also helps us engage with prisoners to whom that means so much: 'I feel like I've got someone there who wants to help me, for no other reason than wanting to. It made me question why at first, because no one's wanted to help me for nothing before.' We do not duplicate nor replace any other services, however, coaching's eclectic development means it incorporates techniques others might use.

Coaching is not a complete solution but it can be an ideal start or boost. We are part of a raft of services available to women in Styal. As a client put it: 'I've never had help before but since coming in here there's loads.' Agencies collaborating with each other is vital. The impact of coaching would be far smaller without all the other support offered in the prison. Our not referring clients to other services stands out, but is an essential part of empowering women to act as their own key-worker and speak for themselves. Coaching gives the client the ability to know their own mind and ask for or find the help they need. We are a blank canvas with enormous flexibility to meet women's needs. 'Coaching is more personal to me and my situation rather than in general, than dealing with everyone in the same basket.' We know it's a luxury to be able to spend an uninterrupted hour or hour and a half working one to one with a prisoner. We are also very aware we only coach the well and the willing, while many in prison are neither.

Coaching fits within the general movement in the prison and criminology circles towards encouraging and mentoring, rather than policing and telling. 'Desistance' essentially means the process of stopping committing crime and there are strong parallels between our approach and what researchers have found works, such as working with people as individuals in a positive, motivational way. CIAO's approach is epitomized by the woman who said: 'Thank you so much for calling us clients'. When a prison number (like A1234XY) is substituted for your name, it really matters how you are described. We call those we work with 'clients' because we coach individuals as people, not prisoners. So, it was natural to use the same term I would use coaching anyone.

From the start, governors saw it as essential for CIAO to be operating 'independently from the prison and having some sort of deliberate firewalls in place…So it wasn't seen as being a prison scheme; it was seen as an external scheme coming in'. We do not even attempt to influence the system by acting as referees or advocates, regardless of what we may think or believe about a client. Coaches do not know and cannot judge if a prisoner will commit another crime, nor do we want that authority. That is the very opposite of our role. We have a sense of who clients are but do not know them. We are only with them for very short periods of time. We do not prepare clients for any court hearings or prison meetings, such as parole boards. If a client says they are innocent, which has happened more than once, we neither dispute nor agree with this. Instead, we explain anything relating to their conviction is for them to explore elsewhere.

We complement the probation service and have helped improve some clients' working relationships with them. A probation officer said: 'It was wonderful to see both these women with a sparkle in their eye and with a true belief that they could have a worthwhile future.' She believed coaching:

> has given both these women the opportunity to concentrate on themselves as individuals rather than just focusing on the reduction of risk/the offence, which is obviously what I have to do. A byproduct of this is that they have reduced their risk levels, as they now have a renewed belief in themselves which is a great protective factor.

Another added: 'People perceive the probation relationship as judgemental or labelling; you're with an authority figure and respond accordingly…[whereas with coaching] there's no forcing, you're there because you want to be and recognize the value of it.'

Most prisoners are asked to do courses to address their behaviour and there are nearly 50 of these different Accredited Offending Behaviour Programmes to help prepare them for release on one Ministry of Justice web page alone. Doing a course like the 'Thinking Skills Programme' and coaching at the same time can be akin to when I tried to learn Spanish and Italian and my brain was just too full, but some clients find a simultaneous approach works well. For one: 'The coaching chimed perfectly with a victim awareness course.' It is all down to the individual, and coaches are sensitive to this.

Independent research showed CIAO's coaching 'helped [clients] to get more out of other interventions and/or encouraged them to apply for other programmes and schemes, to take their progress further' with clients saying, 'I've had a better understanding of a lot of the courses I've done here; I really have' and, 'Having done coaching, I can do these various packages and work out my own package from them.'

Sorry, what was your name again?

Our systems are designed so that the most anyone can find out from our records about a particular woman in Styal is that we are coaching her, and even finding that out would mean hacking into secure electronic systems. There is irony in CIAO using ID numbers when we are so dedicated to treating clients as individuals, though, and this does make it easier to forget names. Or, if you do remember names and don't write down prison numbers, it can cause a comedy of errors. We have tried to coach the wrong JK not once but twice, as two women in the prison had exactly the same name, so another baffled JK turned up a second time, while the woman who actually wanted coaching patiently waited a little longer.

We look after ourselves too. Coaches only use first names but, not being so bright, I completed a signing-in sheet in full once and my 'cat sat on the mat' writing and signature clearly showed my surname to anyone who cared to read it. Now we just initial them to keep our surnames confidential. Realistically, anyone can work out who I am extremely quickly as soon as they look online, so I'm no longer concerned about that; however, protecting the other coaches remains important.

We are wary of any information we give out. Even simple things such as whether or not you have children can lead to manipulation if you unwittingly give out details that make it possible for prisoners, not necessarily your own clients, to work out where they go to school. This is one reason why when a client did eventually ask, after nearly a year and a half, whether I had children, I asked her: 'Would it make any difference either way?' We keep the focus of coaching on the client, not the coach.

We ask all clients' permission to discuss their coaching within CIAO, using only first names, and to share stories and quotes outside the group in a way that does not identify them. This is so we can support our coaches and clients as far as possible and to enable us to promote coaching. We ask if we can take notes and offer to show the client anything we do write down. Our touchstone is that notes do not identify anyone and we would happily leave them on a bus or hand them over to a journalist. The other key test is: 'What if a victim saw these notes?' However, writing up notes afterwards is important for many coaches: 'Writing up sessions is when I appreciate what we've done. I don't know what they've done until then.'

You'll note that in saying this the coach changed the pronoun from 'we' to 'they', even while describing the effect, to ensure the client, not the coach, received the credit.

As well as respecting coaching confidentiality, all the coaches have signed the Official Secrets Act and we take the privilege of our position seriously, including being very careful with information we may have gathered or simply learnt about within the prison. Coincidences happen and we have to protect against this. Years ago as a consultant I was shown a file in Strangeways to illustrate how an employment service worked and it turned out to be that of the young man who tried to steal my wallet at Piccadilly station the year before. I did not even know he was in prison, let alone in Manchester. It was all I could do to stop myself writing to him to ask how he was now and what situation he had been in then.

Security does mean everything takes longer than working with professional clients and things can occasionally be too safe for their own good. I once emailed my criminal justice account from my normal one and it bounced back as 'Sender address belongs to a non-trusted organization.' Telling my laptop: 'But it's me!' had little effect. Another coach was locked out of a prison computer, which had already taken half an hour to 'verify' her, and was told: 'You can't leave now!' So she had to wait for it to be resolved before she could log out and leave the system secure.

Being in prison in any sense affects who you are on many levels. It makes you zen or pushes you to your limits. Sometimes on the very same day.

8 What helps you?

What coaches do is simple yet clever and coaching can have a very deep impact. When someone asked me: 'Why does coaching resonate with human beings?' I realized that it is because it is entirely about them.

What follows is not all that we do in CIAO, nor exactly how we do it, but it outlines how we both challenge and support our clients. This glimpse into techniques and ideas also highlights how much I have to learn and explore, but you do not need to be the best coach ever to help someone. At the start I would go into the prison armed with pages of notes but I now know I work best when I have confidence in both my client and in me, so I trust myself and wing it. Complex techniques can always be helped by the simple request: 'Tell me more...'

Confidence and confidentiality

Some women in Styal have no trust or their past trust has been badly misplaced, so we don't *ask* them to trust us. I simply *expect* my clients to, and wait for that to happen when they're ready. Trust is very emotive in prison, where you can be vulnerable if you are too trusting and many say, 'I don't trust anybody in here.' Coaches work hard to get their clients in a different place, not least with the Star and the all-important crossing out of 'Offending'. We then stand a better chance of lessening the defensiveness of women who can anticipate their version of the truth will be disputed. Clients in prison have said they can 'drop the bravado'. One coach commented: 'coaching had given her the strength to be honest and the space to express underlying problems: shown her how to ask for help and changed her life around'. Some open up more readily: 'They can cut to the chase much more than professional clients.' This may be the relief of being able to put down the burden of keeping thoughts and fears to yourself.

All types of clients tell me: 'I've never told anyone this…' Em telling me something she had never told anyone else in the prison within an hour of walking into the room went even further. Opening up and sharing things people have never said before can happen in a safe and almost totally confidential space because, as one client said, of 'feeling very valued and listened to'. Others said of their coaches:

> a match made in heaven…to make a connection as strong as I feel that I got from that coaching…they're very clever at what they do, the way they make you open up more; just put you at ease perhaps.

And, 'It was just so comfortable to be round that person.' It is not always comfortable though. A professional client told me: 'I feel like I'm going for brain surgery while awake.'

We have confidence in our clients, many of whom have been told that they are stupid or useless, whereas we truly believe they are worth listening to and are capable of change. Our ground rules set out this respect and expectation in writing, as well as our embodying it throughout. We also make it explicit that the coach has no agenda other than the best interests of the client.

Some managers and other staff in prison are trained as coaches to help one another develop. In some other prisons staff have been trained to coach prisoners too. However, one of our clients captured the difference in strangers volunteering to come in from outside:

> You're doing some coaching with someone qualified, is willing to listen to you; somebody that you can put a bit more trust into. It's not somebody within the prison because I think you're very limited on whatever you can say and whatever in here, because nothing's private really. So, with somebody coming in I think you can be a bit more relaxed. You can be a bit more open with them because they're not in here and with the confidentiality thing I think there's more trust there I think as well. I'm not saying the prison's a bad place but obviously some things can be repeated within here which could cause you more stress, but with coaching I think it's a bit more private. And that in itself, I think that's great, that they volunteer to come in and do that with people.

It can also be a different relationship because of the power and responsibilities other organizations have: 'She doesn't want to tell other bodies what she really thinks, as this can have implications.' I have seen clients start from a position of conflict with their head down and then lift it the moment the member of staff left the room. They say of CIAO:

They treated me like any other person, as if we weren't here in a prison environment. I could have been going to their offices seeing them. It just made not the slightest bit of difference at all... it was great.

Trust is still not always immediate though:

I felt that S was assessing me and the coaching process during the first session and I was unsure about whether she was telling me the whole truth or just what she felt was the correct thing to say to get her positioned best when the feedback got back to the prison. On reflection I now believe that there may have been a little of that in that first session but from then on she was focused solely on what would benefit her for the future and was open and honest (both I and the process must have passed her test!).

Respectful uncertainty: who are we to judge?

Our confidence is not limitless either and we are still tested at times. Once I stood waiting at the bottom of some stairs and heard a client adopting a totally different character and wondered 'Am I being played?' This was as near as I have been to disliking any client and I was very curious about my reaction. I was annoyed at waiting yet again, as it was clear she was definitely not doing her utmost to be on time, even though punctuality was something she had chosen to work on. My irritation also stemmed from many hours of waiting for clients over the months, coinciding with an apparent lack of excuses. Our clients do not have to earn their coach's respect, though, we give that automatically. However, we can never be absolutely sure of anything with anyone. Even then I could not be sure she was not just showing off, putting up a facade or exerting what little power she had in prison.

Fortunately there is also no need for us to be certain about what we are told because that is not the point of coaching. We are not analysing clients and submitting a report. We are there for their benefit, not ours. This is why the concept of 'respectful uncertainty' is so useful. When I am unsure of something someone is saying, often because I think they may be deluding themselves far more than trying to mislead me, I can simply work with it while holding down my eyebrows and biting back any temptation to say: 'Really???' It is better to let the thoughts pass and remain curious in the moment, rather than judging. It is for clients to make sense of their lives, not the coaches. We can simply trust clients within sessions. Things may not be true for all sorts of reasons, not necessarily because the client knows they are not true, or: 'She may be telling me what she thinks I will want to hear...'

Clients may be taking advantage for reasons we don't know or understand, but with respectful uncertainty that isn't a problem. Coaches hold that tension in themselves and, as we do so, a client can realize the benefits to them and change their approach to coaching. We have no incentive to be drawn in by clients who are simply looking for short-term rewards. As we are careful not to act on anything we are told, other than risk of harm to the client or others, there is no risk in doing this. Coaching can be like filming a documentary, where participants' awareness of the camera fades and they become themselves after a while. By trusting the client and working with uncertainty we increase the chances of this epiphany.

Our clients have all been judged by someone put in a position of authority to do just that. My instinct is to trust and think the best of people. I am very open and do not put my guard up. I see the good in others far more than their flaws. It is harder if you are judgemental – even if you can hide your prejudices verbally, your face and body language may give much away.

As a coach who sits on the bench said:

> I am learning about life in prison...and that *all* people are capable of change...It has had a huge impact on me personally. I have only seen the criminal justice system at work previously from the sentencing side as a magistrate and inevitably one becomes a little cynical, seeing only the failures of the system, rather than any successes. This view meant that – at first – I could see little hope of real change in my client (or possibly any client) and therefore felt 'stuck' after the initial sessions and sought feedback and help from my peer mentor. I realize now that I was coming from an 'I'm OK / You're not OK' position and judging my client, rather than from a position of unconditional positive regard.

This coach, who is a magistrate, being open enough to say 'I am learning not to be so judgemental!' was another highlight of how much we have all grown and how open we are about that growth.

Our aim of working as equals is helped by our choosing to have no authority nor any desire to influence prisoners' lives in ways other than those they choose. If you foolishly think someone is inferior to you the chances are they know it, consciously or subconsciously. '[My coach] never, ever judged and I think that's very important for people in this situation, to feel that you are never judged, and she never, ever did.' Judging people after they have been judged by the criminal justice system, as we all inevitably do, holds us back and restricts society from reaching its potential. I do my utmost to let go of any negative reaction that crosses my mind so that I live up to the view of my professional client who said:

'It is nice to be able to admit weaknesses without being judged.' Coaches learn to trust the power of coaching too:

> I went into every session worried about the impact I was having and whether I was having any impact at all, however... she was finding the sessions very useful and would not have been able to achieve what she had done without the non-judgemental approach.

It works both ways though, and first impressions might be barriers to being coached in the first place. A friend of CIAO's who was once a prisoner in Styal spoke of clients judging coaches by their jewellery and being able to smell their 'expensive perfume' and 'Garnier face cream'. She was clearly not talking about me, though, as washing my face is the highlight of my beauty regime. These instant human judgements are one of many reasons that what previous clients say to others is so essential to our continuing work.

Listen very carefully...

Listening to every word and nuance is essential and listening on the very simplest level can also have a huge impact. Nothing is the same as someone else paying you attention and concentrating solely on you: challenging, pushing and supporting. Often no one has really listened to our clients for five minutes, let alone six hours: 'They respond to someone who is paying them attention and wants them to talk and wants them to say more.' As a client said: 'You allowed me to explore myself... to vocally speak up instead of internalizing... things sound different out loud.'

Clients are listened to while they reflect on and talk about their lives, sometimes for the first time. Things can make more sense and you can see what you're thinking. When the coach plays words back it can be even clearer: 'Hearing someone else say what's been going round in your head is totally different.' This is even more vital in a place where a client said: 'Nobody listens to me except you.' We listen for patterns and repetition in clients' behaviour and state, as well as their language, and look out for when people are stuck. Hearing what isn't being said and being careful to clarify meaning rather than assuming we understand is key. 'It was good for me to speak out my jumbled thoughts. You have helped me put them in some order.'

Watching for clues is equally central, as our bodies can say so much more than words – from subtle eye movements to the bloody manifestation of inner pain. I do not analyse this in textbook fashion, I just listen to how I feel. I learnt most of what I know about body language from months living and working with a woman who was severely autistic and could not speak. It is amazing what you see when you shut up and listen. Watching is not the coaches' prerogative either. Clients can watch for clues as to the answers they think the coach may want, particularly when some still think there is a 'right answer' or a 'test' for them to 'pass'. This is much more the case than with my professional clients, though not uniquely so.

However much we may try to act as equals, some clients will always see us as being in a position of authority. It is not just a matter of avoiding questions which are judgements in disguise but also of counteracting decades of clients' experience of questions that are meant negatively. This is not just the case in the prison. It was a professional client to whom I felt I had to say: 'Nothing I say will be meant as a criticism and there is no need to apologize. I will only ask you a question because I'm really curious about the answer, not to make a point.'

The physical changes we see can be transformational, as Em showed. Someone else's client, with whom I had worked briefly, had changed so much I failed to recognize her a few months later. One coach almost walked by his own client when he bumped into her in smart clothes and make-up returning to the prison after a day working in the community. She thrilled him by saying: 'It was really lovely meeting with you and working with you. I'll see you again.'

Questions, questions

Questioning is probably the most powerful thing we do, after keeping quiet. Listening may be essential but coaching is about exploration and thinking the unthought. Timely questions can increase personal awareness and trigger a realization or shift in perception, without the coach even knowing or needing to hear the answer. Insights gained by the client are more important than any stumbled upon by the coach. We are interested in questions that make people think differently, not just those they know the answer to but we do not. This can be particularly hard and particularly rewarding when, at first, many of our clients lack the belief that they have any answers at all.

One of my approaches with strangers in life involves questions that establish common interests, as well as enjoying the conversation itself: my husband calls it research for *Clare's Book of Facts*. This is totally inappropriate for coaching, though, as it as much about me as the other person. This shift to asking questions for the client's benefit, not yours, can be even harder when you may be curious about their past, as you know they have transgressed to be in prison. This makes it even more essential to check why you are asking a question and ensure questions you do ask are to help the client. Coaching is not about the details of the client's problem or their history, they are very familiar with those already. It is about helping them reconsider the way they are looking at the problem and all the options they may have. Clients are often able to take this questioning approach away with them for the future: 'Without the coaching I wouldn't have been able to ask myself the right questions or think things through.'

Helping clients find the right language to express themselves and make sense of their thoughts and feelings, while doing our utmost to ensure that the final version is their words not ours, is a real joy. It was a professional client who said a while ago: 'You have really effective articulation. That's the beauty of working with someone like you. You are very perceptive. You see things I am trying to say before I find words to say them myself.' However, I no longer indulge my love of words and try to give a client more time to find the phrase that suits them instead. I am much happier that a Styal client said of our coaching: 'It doesn't put words into your mouth.' Putting thoughts into words leaves us open to challenge but helps us work things out, if we are brave enough to admit them. Emotions dam up my words, which can be initially frustrating and then overwhelming, but the pressure eventually forces out a rush of coherence if someone is patient enough to wait for me to speak.

Clients do not always need to know why they think or act a certain way. I am highly analytical: the kind of person who looks back and logs their time spent on various projects to the nearest six minutes. This began back when I first became self-employed and I was baffled as to why I was so exhausted, as my 'billable hours' seemed normal. Then, when I recorded all my time, I realized how much background thinking and networking made it all happen. The result was I was still exhausted but I was happily clear about the cause, which was all I needed. However, for most people, simply analysing and understanding why something is the case is not enough and sometimes not even helpful.

Realizing a new pattern can be created, if the approach a client uses to help them function no longer serves them well, is the true breakthrough. We all do things based on what we know and feel at the time. That does not mean we should stick with a process that doesn't work for us any more or, indeed, never worked. Thinking is our attempt to understand behaviour, not the real explanation for it. If you ask 'Why did that happen?' the reply is an interpretation, whereas if you ask 'What happened?' you're more likely to get the facts. Interpretations can reinforce what a client already thinks, within the old frame of reference that limits their view, rather than opening up more options. The question 'Why?' is most useful to hear how someone thinks and expresses themselves, not to hear what they think or feel.

Drawing out understanding happens in both senses too: through asking questions and through putting pen to paper. Occasionally I scribble pictures with a greater tendency to amuse than illuminate, but some clients like both the thinking time and the creativity of being able to sketch or 'mind map', as well as to speak.

The matrix

To get different perspectives and explore motivation towards a goal I often ask clients to complete a matrix to map out what might be lost or gained from sticking with the status quo or changing. On the left are things as they are and the potential future is on the right. At the top are the good points of each situation and the bad points below. My questions to fill the four quadrants are the four variations on: 'What is the best/worst thing that could happen if you did/didn't do this?' followed by: 'What other good or bad things could happen?' This can show if achieving the goal may mean losing positive elements of a current position, which might subconsciously limit striving towards that goal or really annoy you if you only realized it later. It can also prompt action as the reality of a very negative situation becomes clearer. Asking 'What might be stopping you from starting or doing this?' and 'Who do you want to change for?' can help too.

I used this approach to explore being late for appointments with Akshata. Discussing how she might get to work and other appointments on time when in the community, shifted from buying herself a bike to leaving earlier and multi-tasking by brushing her teeth in the bath. She gained nothing by being late but lost out by being annoyed at missing the appointment, even though she put the same effort into travelling as she would put into getting there on time. If on time she would be 'happy, successful and amazed' and all she lost was the possibility of missing something important on the news. A coaching triumph was her weighing up the cost of a bike and the likelihood of a puncture against the benefit of watching a few more minutes of Jeremy Kyle. She reached the conclusion that Mr Kyle is not worth it and she may as well walk.

It was during this discussion about how she used her time that I glanced up to see a clock on the wall stuck at thirteen minutes to seven. The second hand quivered but did not have enough energy to make the leap. The next session we were delighted to see the battery had been changed. Time standing still in a prison was a metaphor too far.

Points of view

When struggling with people, many of my clients have explored the different options and outcomes prompted by the four possibilities of doing nothing or changing one of three things: you, them or the situation. Realizing you can simply change your view of the problem can be liberating. Looking at triggers and reinforcements of the situation has also helped. Exploring anger at someone can show what we are at odds with within ourselves too, as others often reflect us and the things that we find most annoying can be our own biggest flaws.

How other people might see the client (or the situation a client is in) differently can be a simple matter of asking the question. Some clients respond to being asked: 'What advice would you give a friend? Where should she start?' Even: 'Tell me, what am I thinking?' can be a useful extra nudge to help them look at it from another perspective that 'helps you see things from different angles'.

Taking this shift in perspectives further, I have worked with clients to look at their relationships using the 'positions' and 'empty chair' approaches. This is when I also often remind clients that they agreed to suspend their disbelief in coaching and try out activities that might take them outside their comfort zones.

Louise and I were in one of the airy dining rooms with radiators barely visible under drying clothes. In between the set meal times it was possible to find an hour or so to coach, as long as you did not mind people occasionally coming in to use the toaster or microwave to supplement prison menus with food they had bought themselves. I scraped the lightweight chairs around the table, so that one was for Louise, another for her family and another where she might imagine seeing her interaction with her family as if an outsider. Sitting in the different positions and looking back at the empty chairs in which she had sat helped her understand both her reactions to others and how she might think and act differently, so that everyone could get on better. Louise became curious why people act the way they do and realized sometimes her problem was with herself, not others. Both she and I were stunned at how well this worked. Sometimes the coach is suspending their disbelief just as much as the client.

Sounding board or echo chamber?

Challenging responses and actions is critical in all senses, particularly when we think a client may be fooling herself. All my clients from every walk of life appreciate challenge, but how you do it is key. We all fool ourselves at times, so holding up a mirror to your client's contradictions or inconsistencies is no judgement: 'It helps you to think about why you are behaving or thinking as you do, and helps you to re-think.' The sounding board of coaching can become a mere echo chamber, or even collusion, if challenge is missing. Hearing our own words without a mindless affirmation can help us see the reality, or occasional lunacy, behind them: 'I step back and look at myself from a different angle. Talking about it is part of the process of understanding it myself.'

This is probably the element I tailor most carefully to the individual – working out when to ask clients if they're ready to decide or act, or allowing them to reflect and choose their pace with a nudge, further exploration, or more robust challenge if it feels right. Some professionals are upfront about their sensitivity or what they're looking for: 'I want you to challenge me in a way that does not damage my large but sensitive ego.' One was even more clear: 'I want you to tell me I'm right to have decided to quit my job.' This is much less common in the prison.

Giving honest feedback and challenging women proved harder for some coaches, as three told me:

> I am learning all the time – especially to be more focused on challenge and outcomes. Don't just sit and 'listen', however important 'empathy' and 'listening' are as skills.
>
> She talked of the sessions as being very different from counselling, where someone just listened to her moaning... maybe that meant I am getting better at the challenge part of coaching.
>
> Last time I didn't challenge. I felt I shouldn't challenge as much as they don't have the capacity within them to think. But they do. I'd challenge a manager and it would be patronizing not to challenge a woman in Styal. But they actually like being challenged and come up with answers themselves.

If it feels someone is not getting anywhere with a goal it can help to ask: 'Why are you fighting what you say you want? Is this a good goal for you at this time?' As long as a client is sure it is something they really want then a goal that may seem beyond them right now is worth struggling with. However, if they realize it is not one they care enough about to take seriously or fight for, then letting go of it frees them up to use that energy elsewhere and accept the consequences of that decision.

Decisions themselves take up our energy too. Outside the prison, when a client has been uncertain for a while and struggling to make a binary decision, I sometimes put a 10p coin I found outside a probation office between us. The provocation of saying I will just flip it introduces uncertainty that can then be resolved one way or another. The point is not the outcome itself but their reaction to it. This can be enough to tell them whether that was what they wanted after all or to prompt other reflections.

Holding the tension

The power of coaching lies in the tension you create for the client. Silence and biting your tongue are two of the hardest things client and coach have to deal with, but they work. Interruptions should be to open up new avenues to learn about the client, not the situation. While not knowing the system helps prevent you trying to come up with solutions for your client, it does help to know something of the ubiquitous prison slang and jargon. I often think hard whether interrupting to satisfy my curiosity about what something means would really outweigh derailing the client's train of thought and I try to ask only on a 'need to know' basis. It can also be more difficult for someone to coach who knows the prison or wider criminal justice system, because they have to bite their tongue even harder: 'I have to continually resist my desire to provide answers.' Equally I would never slip into mentoring with a CIAO client, while I may with a professional one if they explicitly ask my advice and I am sure my knowledge or experience, rather than my opinion, might be useful.

Silence encourages the client to speak and, more importantly, to think. As a client said: 'She doesn't tell me – she sits there and makes you think of it yourself.' It allows me to collect my own thoughts too and I am happy to wait quietly for as long as it takes for them to be ready. Another coach said: 'When the client asks a question they hear it for themselves and begin to think about and answer it when they see/realize the question is hanging there and an answer won't come from anywhere else.'

The tension can also come from holding up two things that seem to conflict and asking the client how they would reconcile them. For instance, how they are currently behaving and their goals – i.e. the gap between where the client is now and where they want to be. It is for the client to consider how their current path may not be taking them where they want to go, not for the coach to point out a mismatch.

Only the client knows what is really true and best for them. If they say 'I don't know' you may have been too direct or moved too fast, too soon. It can help to indicate that you are happy to wait: 'When do you think you will know?' Or they may need encouragement to realize it: 'What if you did know, then what might the answer be?' Similarly, closed questions are often used more when people are trying to move things swiftly on and clients can recognize this as meaning more structured questions will follow at the coach's initiative. Too many closed questions can thus reduce a client's feeling of responsibility and stem their thought flow. That said, I never think systematically about the type of question I'm asking; I just ask what feels right and often that works.

Supporting strengths

No challenge would work without encouraging our clients to set off and keep moving forward on what can be the hardest path they ever take: the one they consciously create and choose for themselves. In prison, even success is poignant and setbacks can hit hard. Rebecca talked about how tough it is to move even a tiny bit when you are in a rut and I reflected how pushing off is the hardest, wobbliest and scariest part about riding a bike. After that it gets easier. This metaphor suited another coach's client too: 'Wouldn't have done it without you – you gave me the first push.' Support can be putting your hands out instinctively to catch someone falling or voluntarily giving someone a leg-up. Coaches sometimes have to catch and steady someone who is crashing, before we are able to get them back where they belong. Officially we do not offer a crisis service, however the level of each client's need is not always apparent at the start.

We build clients' belief and resilience by going with them into areas they might not be willing or feel able to explore on their own: 'this process can help clients to discover resources, strengths and abilities which they would not previously have considered themselves to possess. They find they have a previously unsuspected capacity to tackle issues in their life'. We acknowledge change can be difficult but do not assume this nor guess our client's likely reaction. Prisoners in Styal have often made unenviably tough decisions about their lives. Most of the clients I have worked with have had remarkable heart and courage.

I have never coached any professional client felt to be underperforming, just people who want to develop their strengths and progress still further. This is how CIAO uses coaching too. Some professional clients and customers are reassured by jargon and serious-sounding terminology such as our coaches taking a 'strengths-based' approach. However, the friend I spoke to about focusing on strengths said: 'You're the epitome of how that can work. With all your weaknesses, it's impressive how you get anything done.'

We enable people to reach their potential, rather than look at where others feel they may be going wrong. We also help them find out and build on their abilities: 'it was helping me to deal with my issues, but by myself, by using my own strengths... That's important because you need to be able to deal with things yourself'.

'What's good in here?'

If you want to change anything about yourself in your life change your thoughts. If I'm feeling upset and angry I ask myself what I'm thinking and then change that thought... visualizing a happy time or playing uplifting music. I've noticed that is impossible to feel bad when I have good thoughts. I cannot change past events and there are lots I wouldn't want to. I aim to reflect on positive events that have happened and are happening in the here and now.

In among all the work we do uncovering values and setting goals around the different areas of clients' lives, we explore what there is to appreciate about life as it is. An exercise designed by Martin Seligman, the grandfather of positive psychology, is one I do with most clients. You simply look for and write down Three Good Things, big or small, that have happened at the end of every day for a week. The critical element is also to consider and record why they happened.

Em's initial reaction to this idea was typical: 'I was panicking at first. "I'm in prison: what's good in here?" And you said: "Look for it." And I did… I woke up feeling positive about my life.' Clients see how some good and bad things happened for no reason and no one was responsible. However, a lot of good things happen because of something you do – to the extent that one prisoner said: 'I'm starting to look out for good things to do and make happen.' Actual responses included: 'I had my hair cut for free because she's a nice person and likes me' and 'I was let off work early because the paint ran out.'

A professional client who repeatedly missed out 'why', said there was a 'risk of getting a big head when you don't quite deserve it' and this is the element I have to tease out most often. Though a Styal client could say:

> The Three Good Things made my confidence grow and made me feel that not everybody hates me. I slept better from when I started doing the Three Good Things a day. It's all right someone sayin' nice things but it goes in one ear and out the other but if you write them down you actually see it in black and white.

Two others developed 'learned optimism' – the opposite of what psychologists call 'learned helplessness' – and that it was not the case that 'whatever I do it turns out badly'. They said:

> A lot more things have gone good for me since. I did more things and got positive things back. I used to think I could just sit around and wait for good things to happen… It's just little, tiny things. Imagine if I carried on all the way.

And, 'It started out being more random things I was noticing but now it's things prompted by me. I realized it wasn't other people's advice that was doing it. It was me doing it.' This client got so much from the exercise that now she does it 'whenever I get a bad feeling, not just last thing at night'.

We might suggest concepts too, so I mentioned the idea of 'chaining' her actions together to a client who was forgetting to write down Three Good Things just before going to sleep every day. Deliberately linking a new action to an old one seemed sensible, so I suggested thinking about them while she brushed her teeth. She looked at me as if I was an idiot and explained she brushed her teeth hours before she went to bed and wrote her diary. She was right, of course. I had forgotten (yet again) the many flaws in trying to come up with other people's solutions for them.

How to be psychic

Superstition and belief in the supernatural are common in Styal. A member of staff once told me a client 'thinks you're psychic'. Yet, the answer to the common question 'How did you know?' is often that someone said it but did not hear their own words. The same client thought I was trying to read her 'aura' at one point. I was puzzled when the same issue arose as I was seeking insurance quotes while we were still working completely without payment. When the broker said 'Are you a psychic group?' I burst out laughing and asked why on earth he thought that. Apparently psychics do not get paid either.

Anyone can be 'psychic', it's not even about intuition: just watch, listen and remember. We don't pretend to be mind-readers, nor particularly aim to see our client's point of view. Empathy is much more useful than sympathy. There is definitely something surreal in what we do though. When a client said: 'I drive myself nuts trying to change stuff but when I slow down stuff happens like magic' I replied 'It's not magic. It's you. Work out your part in that and you've cracked it.' The zen response came back: 'learning to just be will help.'

Wrapping up

The final thing we do is to wrap up all that a client has explored and achieved. If everything goes as planned and we know when the last session is and our client isn't transferred out that morning, then we explore strategies for after coaching ends. We ask: 'If you need support who can you ask? Can you tell them your plans? Will they hold you to account? Can you bounce ideas off them?' One client asked if she could pay her coach a retainer on release. The answer was definitely no, but we do offer clients who are still in the prison three-monthly review sessions for as long as they and their coach think this will help and are able to meet. We also now work with some clients after they're released if we have a contract with the area to which they are returning. Some clients want to show their coach how they have moved on or to thank them. Two client responses to whether they would like to meet again and why were: 'Yes, just to know I'm still okay' and 'To show you it works.' Others want to use the review sessions for coaching, perhaps to prepare for imminent release or, because coaching isn't always 'happy ever after', to look at some current issues. Sessions can be joyous though; one coach described how seeing her clients again was one of the highlights of her Christmas. Long-term prisoners can now also have more coaching after a year or so, if they feel they would benefit from it, just like my professional clients.

Clients appreciate the formal certificate we give them to share with others, including staff, who may want some 'proof' that there was real work and commitment. This was our first:

> Through the process of coaching and her willingness to take up the challenges it presents, Rebecca achieved the following:
>
> * Realised she has all the answers she needs within her
> * Showed a real enthusiasm to change and acted with great courage
> * Developed a desire to be honest with herself and others
> * Devised plans and options, which she developed and tested
> * Gained insights into choices and consequences learnt from her actions.
>
> She also has:
>
> * A family that energizes her and gives her direction
> * The ability and eagerness to fulfil her potential.

Her personal certificate said:

> When we first met you asked: 'What would you do?' before laughing, as you remembered what coaching was all about. That was a great start. You have shown that you know your own answers and you always will. This is your life.
>
> You stunned me when you instantly took steps to change, unprompted. You chose to push, to act courageously, to be honest with yourself and others, and to accept the consequences. You devised plans full of options that you tested and developed, as you learned what works for you.
>
> You have more than enough reasons to be 'full of yourself'.
>
> You know what matters to you and who you are. All that you have discovered is yours to keep. Just remember it's 'rocket science' and that both your energy and your direction come from your family.
>
> I admire you too, Rebecca, and wish you the very best in life.

9   What holds you back?

We all have our own MO, whether that 'modus operandi' is the patterns we repeat in the crimes we commit or our general 'way of doing things' in life. There are many different ways we repeatedly stop ourselves achieving all we can. What do you do when you feel threatened? How do you protect yourself? Coping mechanisms people have developed to survive in what can be the hostile environment of a prison are not always helpful ways of operating in the community or for moving forward more generally. Coaching has helped clients change their behaviour – as one said: 'It's had a massive impact – I could be off the house, off enhanced [privilege status] and down the wing.' This chapter isn't just about dismantling resistance and releasing our clients' potential, it's also about what has held us back in the prison and in ourselves, for good and ill.

Changing your mind

As human beings, we sabotage ourselves all the time and prison may be the pinnacle of this. Limiting beliefs, assumptions or behaviours are therefore the third essential area all coaches address and I have worked just as much on these hidden blockers as on goals clients suggest themselves:

> I knew what I wanted to do and knew that I could try to do them but I just put them all to the back of my mind as I thought that I might fail. I had lots of negative thoughts. Since my coaching I always give things a go. I know that I won't beat myself up if I can't.

When I took much of my personal approach out of our CIAO documents I removed the use of the word 'Gremlin' for the negative inner voice that tells us we are useless. One reason was wariness of talking about hearing voices in prison where mental health problems were common. A professional client loved the concept though and disconcertingly his Gremlin was screaming: 'You're going to have to do this! She's going to ask you if you've done anything!' At least one Gremlin in the world is on my side though. Another coach's client found: 'I've got this new voice in my head that I can guide myself with and it's not going away.'

What is stopping *you*? What we dread or put off most often shrinks dramatically when stared at hard enough. Or, if that doesn't work, what happens if you walk on by barely giving it a sideways glance? Try doubting your Gremlin instead of doubting yourself. As well as the inner voice there is the negative reinforcing we say out loud, such as the client who said: 'I'm not a thinker.' To which I replied: 'Oh you are! It's just easier not to be.' An hour later she was able to joke: 'I'm a potential lifer. We've got plenty of time. My brain might be an issue, however. I didn't think you'd get more than three words. Actually you got loads.'

The way we hold ourselves back consciously or unconsciously can be more fundamental. Sometimes we're not true to who we really are. When a coach asked her client: 'Are you being you?' she burst into tears and said: 'No! I'm absolutely not.' She had acted as someone else for over a decade, hiding her true self, becoming harsher and harsher to punish herself and deal with her vast guilt at her crime.

Changing your mind and turning your beliefs on their head can seem more fanciful in theory than reality. A professional client thought it sounded glib; however, it worked for him too when he suspended his disbelief. The trick is how the magic word 'if' swerves around your subconscious resistance before the Gremlin even realizes something is afoot.

'I didn't know how to think before'

Clients can be held back by their own and others' belief that they are irredeemable and out of control, as well as by the word 'criminal' invisibly branded on their forehead. Independent evaluation has shown many of CIAO's clients come to 'a realization that they could exert control in their own lives, whether in custody or out (or both)'.

> To try and get her to think of any options that she could come up with I asked her: 'What do you have control over?' and then she'd say, well she has control over these choices and then... asking her... more closed questions, like 'Do you have to do just that?'

Lack of self-belief can be so deeply ingrained that a client sometimes cannot realize her own part in the change. For one woman her coach said: 'Each time the problem was solved and she had no idea how.'

Staff said one client 'wants to achieve and make prison work for her'. She went from being 'the squeaky mouse in the corner' to taking lead responsibility for a high-profile project within the prison and attending national conferences on day release. She wrote to her family about the impact of things they had done to her in the past, gave up smoking and created a 'mind map' plan to secure a job in radio:

> I wouldn't be the person I am now...It has motivated me to do things...Prison makes you think a lot, but I didn't know how to think before – I wouldn't have got anywhere without the life coaching....I didn't understand myself before.

Looking at how a negative belief such as 'I am a victim in all this' serves the client can also unearth why someone may behave in a particular way. For example, giving up control and feeling a victim is a ready-made excuse to be angry with others and not accountable, nor do you have to change anything about yourself. Yet changing ourselves is generally a lot easier than changing other people. Blame as a way of projecting and discharging our internal pain and discomfort onto others is a useful way for me to understand behaviour, not least my own. There is a great deal of pain in the prison and coaching can help deal with this, so clients can look to the future:

> It was fantastic. I've learned to put the past behind me and move on. I've changed myself so much in here. I was very bitter at one time...I had a lot of hurt going on inside.

Limiting beliefs and behaviours do not have to be deeply destructive to hold us back. Even while writing this book I realized I happily spend money on others, but not on me, and wondered about that. The trigger was the discrepancy between my willingness to give to charities and to support CIAO for years, while not paying £28 for book-writing software that would make my life far easier. A friend's suggestions of 'Unstinting selflessness? Embarrassment of (your) riches?' were less true than hair-shirtedness and idiotic bloodymindedness. Doing as much as I can with very little is also something of a game for me. This may also stem from not always having money and being very slow to adjust.

That realization helped me to decide I was now going to buy anything that seemed useful. My flawed belief had been that: 'I help others, not me, even if helping me might mean I can help others more.' That response in a text exchange helped me pin down my problem. It is about knowing how investing in me could benefit others. I might even spoil myself occasionally now too, by which I mean replace those shoes that have holes in: best not take things too far. However ridiculous this may sound, that was all I needed to give myself permission to act in a very different way and that really is how it can work for our clients too.

'He who opts for revenge should dig two graves'

Sarah came to an early group session because she wanted another certificate for her collection. In our one-to-one session we explored this need, looking at it as if it were no longer the case, and she turned it into the new positive belief: 'I know when I've done well and don't need certificates to prove that.' Yet this felt empty with none of the release of energy that comes when a client gets to the heart of their problem, so I said: 'That's not it, is it? There's something else.' She agreed and nearly broke down as she slowly admitted she did not believe she could be a good mum because of the guilt she felt at trying to kill herself. She did not believe she was worthy of her children's love. We were close to tears as we discussed this and all she might do to be as good a mother as she could possibly be from within the prison. We eventually sat staring at these slightly blurred words: 'I'm valuable and here are five reasons why: I'm a good listener, caring, non-judgemental, helpful and (most importantly) a good mum.'

The next time we met everything had changed and Sarah later wrote:

> For six months I had only seen my children twice, as I didn't have the nerve to ring my ex-husband and ask could I ring them. After my first session I got the courage to ask and he agreed no problem. I can now speak to my children. They are now always at the phone waiting to hear from me on a Friday evening. I know all that's happened to them that week. To Clare I will always be truly thankful for this.

To turn around her certificate obsession we agreed I would only give her one if she failed at something. So she opted to stop biting her nails, as she never managed that for long. Her treat was to buy Tetley tea bags if she managed it 'because I'm worth it and I can'. Sarah never did get that certificate. She grew her nails instead and said:

> I think I've changed loads. I've lost four pounds in three weeks. I've switched to saving £3 a week that used to go on rubbish like chocolate and crisps. I still allow myself treats, for instance I buy myself bubble bath and on Thursdays I have crumble and custard. It turns out I'm not that keen on Tetley.

She later did an NVQ for the credits alone and her certificates are not even up on the wall: 'They're in a file under my bed and very rarely come out. Not for ages.' More importantly though, as we saw earlier and Sarah said later, she is now 'a good mum who was in a very bad place'.

Sarah went even further over the months that we kept in touch while she was still in Styal.

> I've done a victim awareness course but it's been very hard [because there was no conventional victim]. Instead I have to forgive myself. I've forgiven myself now and I've forgiven my uncle [who abused her when she was young]. He's gone. He's nothing to me.

She said the Chinese proverb, *'He who opts for revenge should dig two graves'* struck such a chord that 'it's going on my arm'. Choosing a tattoo that visibly released her hurt and resentment was a poignant and positive parallel to the raw slashes on her arms when we first met. When I saw her for the last time she told me: '£56 it'll cost me and it'll go over my scars.'

What held us back externally

Prison staff are paid to be wary and it takes years to learn true 'jailcraft'. Staff have occasionally held us back for our own safety and the safety of others. We have to balance our passion with security and deal with the occasional terror that creates: 'Sorry. What have I done now?' I do wonder just how many internal reports the prison had when we began and am glad they were patient enough to call me late one evening on only one occasion. The power shift of coaching can be scary both for clients and the 'authorities'. We had to build up trust and understanding with everyone. A member of staff who said we were initially seen as that 'airy-fairy lot floating round the prison' added 'I love that coaching can affect the culture from the bottom up.'

An innovative and unconventional group going into the secure environment of a prison presents huge challenges for both parties. Prisons are complex, ever-changing places so coaches need to be able to work in a state of uncertainty and ambiguity. CIAO has required great flexibility with immediate learning and changes from all concerned, including prison staff. Life has not always been smooth. How people dealt with our early mistakes and occasional naivety has really been appreciated by the coaches: 'I've been struck by the helpfulness of the vast majority of prison staff: people who genuinely care about the women.'

Coaches have gone through doors and gates some were terrified of: 'It's taken away my fear of setting foot in a prison environment... I was surprised at how normal it felt' and 'It takes me out of my comfort zone a lot and it's a whole different culture. It's really strange, it's psychological but I feel restricted in here. The gates shut and I feel I must be on my best behaviour: back straight, "yes sir, no sir". Then I come and start with clients and it all disappears. I could be working with someone anywhere.'

In plate-glass corporate headquarters the client often holds the swipecard to let the coach into the building. Opening gates is a power reversal at Styal, where the coach has the keys. You also let yourself out of corporate buildings, something prisons are much less keen on. While waiting at the gate the notices and signs remind you of the severity of penalties for smuggling drugs and other offences. However, there are thank-you cards stuck up in most staff offices, from women who are grateful for the support they received.

The cold steel handle of a heavy high gate smoothed over the years by many hands clanging it shut reminds you of your responsibility as you shake it to be sure it's locked. This habit transfered to how I close my own front door, much to the detriment of the house's frame. Politeness can seem crushed when you can't hold doors or gates open for everyone and have to tell prisoners you can't let them through, but the coaches have adjusted to this with an apology and a smile.

Not having keys is a profoundly and intentionally disabling experience, as I found out when I got stuck inside at the start. Even our 'conscientious objector' among the coaches, who eschewed the symbolic power imbalance of keys around her waist, has now capitulated. While we have internal gate keys, no one, not even the governing governor, has the keys to the main gate. If anyone ever takes the inner keys out of the prison it is a very expensive mistake, as every single lock opened by them has to be changed. There are also other implications I had not thought about until a friend asked: 'So your value as a hostage is increased because you have keys?' I don't hear my dangling key chain now, whereas early on I was moving in a quiet room when I wondered where the buzzing fly was and realized it was the chain swinging from my waist. Even after we had been given keys it took some of us a while to get to grips with the system. Two new coaches couldn't find their way out and another turned to ask a room full of prisoners: 'Do you know which key opens this door?' to be met with the response 'Err, Miss!'

Anyone going into a prison regularly is vetted and it was disconcerting to learn I cannot prove who I am for 10 months of the year because of my two surnames (legal and professional) and the vagaries of modern billing systems. Coaches' various name formations are something I was once grilled about. Prisons are not keen on people using different names, particularly those who occasionally forget what they themselves are called, like me. You look daft when you appear not to know your own surname. 'Did it change recently?' 'Oh no. I married years ago. But I use both...'

Almost a year after we started I spoke to a full staff meeting of more than 100 people with radios crackling on many of their belts. I began by asking them to put up their hands if they recognized me in my usual outfit, complete with hi-vis jacket. Well over 50 hands went up and about 30 stayed up to indicate they had spoken to me at some point. Eight hands remained stretched as high as possible when I asked if I had caused any trouble for them at some point over the past year, including the deputy governor's.

What's in your bag?

There are many things you should not take into prisons. These are a few I really miss as a coach.

The first is not having a mobile phone, complete with electronic diary, contacts and other information. Instead we have to check and note availability for future sessions in advance. The biggest loss is not being able to ring a client to find out where she is, and even a prison radio will only connect us with staff, not clients.

No laptop means I can't type notes to capture my thoughts as efficiently and swiftly as possible. Not being able to search the internet for ideas or a specific approach between sessions is more of a loss than not having Twitter: the pause before I share anything with the world outside Styal adds to my many safety mechanisms that stop me doing things I might regret. Ensuring no memory sticks lurk in a pocket of your bag, nor documents with your home address or a telephone number on, makes the preparation checklist still longer. Much of this is no real sacrifice but it does add an extra layer of complexity.

I am now careful not to take anything in that I would not like every prisoner to read. As someone who recycles paper, taking in documents printed on the back of my husband's old business accounts was not my cleverest moment. Nor can I just print out emails, as they include at least my email address and who knows what else. Information can be pieced together far more easily than you can imagine, so caution is strongly recommended. Though this is nothing compared to higher security prisons where you can't even have documents with staples in, because of how they can be used.

We also can't take in anything to give our clients, other than a card for a birthday or similar occasion. This can feel harsh, compromising coaches' generosity. However, it is to prevent escalation and manipulation, as clients might ask for more and other prisoners or others' clients might react to such special treatment.

Metal cutlery was my downfall once when I went to a meeting as well as coaching a client. I remembered a knife was unlikely to be welcome but the nefarious uses of the spoon I put in with my salad momentarily escaped me. I had barely lifted it out of my bag before it was politely, but swiftly, taken and replaced with a plastic one. You learn lessons quickly when you see people's eyebrows hit the ceiling. Chewing gum is banned too, as it can disable locks, take moulds of keys and has, no doubt, numerous other purposes I remain oblivious to.

Prison staff have occasionally been worried for us and encourage us to keep our 'prison heads' on. The day staff at the gate referred to 'our coaches' was therefore one of many days I walked away with a big grin on my face. An absolute highlight of all my time in Styal was when I was hugged by someone working on the gate for whom I seemed to create extra work nearly every time she saw me. We were part of the team now.

Threats to kill

We are working in a world where a 'threat to kill' can mean just that. Threats that are generally metaphorical outside can be serious inside. While the client who said 'I'll kill her' was not talking about one of the coaches, it was said with real intent and, therefore, reported to security. Fortunately this was an unusual situation for a coach to find themselves in.

While you are more likely to be near violence inside prison you are not necessarily affected directly by it. However, the prison's personal protection training described how there is potentially a 'threat to life' every time we open a door. This made me stop and admire staff all the more. It also reminded me why I wear hefty boots not kitten heels around Styal.

Prison staff are always outnumbered. The national ratio is nearly five prisoners for each officer. With the odds so heavily weighted you cannot rely on physical power to protect yourself and others in your care. Nor do officers working with women, young offenders or in secure hospitals have batons. I am not lacking in fight. I come from a family of professional trained killers with both grandfathers, my father and five uncles all in the RAF. However, this reality of prison life explains why I once stood in front of the inner gate collecting myself and checking my physical resources were strong enough before I put my key in the lock. I was preparing to go in for the first time since smashing a car's rear windscreen with my chin. My shoulder also put an impressive dent in the car door and, while my bike could be ridden home, I went to A&E in an ambulance. This meant I was that bit more aware of my vulnerability and wanted to be extra sure I felt ready and able to defend myself, if required.

New situations still make me wary, however strong I may feel. The first time I entered the wing through a door that I had never opened I felt a flicker of trepidation, took my sunglasses off and put them in the bag that I moved from across my body onto my shoulder, so that it couldn't be so easily pulled around my neck.

In reality the worst that has ever happened to me is that someone drew herself up to her full height. This matched my usual five feet nine inches and heavy boots gave me an inch or so advantage. Even then I didn't worry how close I was to the emergency call bell, but was aware she was nearer the locked door.

Rachael was fed up the second time I saw her properly, as she didn't see why coaching was needed. Yet this was in the early days when some clients were told to do it as part of their sentence plan. I was happy to stop coaching her immediately, particularly when she said she didn't believe anything could change and one of her values was privacy. I was not happy with being told 'Sign my movement slip', so she could go back to her house rather than to the workshop I picked her up from and said she would return to. My blood pressure rose as she moved to the door and said: 'I'm going anyway.' I was as unhappy being told what to do as she was with my refusal. However, I was the one with the keys. That part was unspoken and I really fought my instinct, holding back mirrored feelings of aggression. I didn't want to leave her in a negative position, however superficially cocky she might seem. The client who said 'I don't think I'm strong enough to show weaknesses' epitomized the reason we need to be cautious about this. Instead I drew myself up to my full height and responded with extreme assertion that we were going back to the workshop together and, eventually, that turned out to be the case.

The idea of defending myself in that situation did not cross my mind then but has since. Give me my brain rather than my brawn to rely on any time. My body does not recover so quickly these days.

What held us back internally

It's always a good sign when I think 'Where on earth am I going with this?' halfway through. Sometimes the thought flickers through my mind, 'Who am I even to attempt to help in such a complex and painful situation?' Walking away is an important option but one we rarely choose in CIAO. Holding the tension and pain for a while is often sufficient for a client to find their own way through. The coach simply stands beside them. It is often after moments when you think you are out of your depth that huge breakthroughs happen. Being lost together with a client can be a scary but great space. This uncertainty of where you're going is a feature of some of the very best sessions I have had with clients inside and out.

We do not always get the polite noises or outward signs our professional clients might give us. It can be hard when a coach feels: 'I want a sign she's happy and wants to be there: smiley, saying thank you or wanting another session... I want to see progress so that I know I'm not wasting my valuable time.' We can all recognize the feeling when a coach said: 'I felt a bit of a failure. I didn't feel able to help or that I'd done the right thing.' However, this also raised the supportive questions from other coaches: 'Effective in whose eyes and by what measure? Whose judgement is working here? Who says they have to resolve anything?' and the point that 'If you're worrying about this you're not really in the right place to help them, particularly when you're asking the client not to have negative voices in their head.'

Occasionally, sharing your doubt and being open with a client about your feelings on how a session went or is going can open up things up still further. The point is that coaches cannot always see their impact. A coach was struggling to know the benefit of what they had done together but his client later said she enjoyed their conversations and gained 'loads' from them. Occasionally we all need to remind ourselves that: 'We give clients time to think. Just turning up may be enough.'

Our own issues can leak out into our work or, as some of CIAO's wise coaches have said: 'Your clients always bring your stuff to you' and 'You're there for a reason too.' Fortunately there is a flip side to this – as another coach said: 'I come out feeling as good as she does.' It intrigues me when I see myself in the mirror of my client, more often on reflection than in the moment, and how we learn about ourselves from coaching. It is particularly intriguing when I see my own flaws reflected or imagined and end up confronting my own thoughts and responses at the same time as clients work out theirs. Annoyance often comes from my similarities with a client winding me up. The effect your strength of feeling has on clients can work in different ways: '(My coach) was positive that something will come from this; I didn't want to disappoint her' or '(My coach) could cheer me up even when I didn't want to be cheered up.'

Particularly repulsive crimes can affect the coach too:

> This has been a difficult client from my point of view. She told me about her crime early on and it revolted me. It was hard to get back to the I'm OK, you're OK standpoint. At one stage I would have liked to stop coaching her but I gave myself a little time in between sessions and this helped... In the end... it all worked out well. We ended by hugging.

A much more awkward situation arose when a coach sensed there was something she was not being told and Googled her client, which we now make very clear is not in anyone's best interests, however natural it has become. Finding out her client had committed an extreme crime led to a discussion with me in the role of a coaching 'buddy'. We were guided by CIAO's principle of working with the person in front of us now, unaffected by their past actions or offences. This meant the coach said nothing to the client, held the tension of her knowledge within her and was rewarded when the client eventually shared her crime. The coach was then able to react with compassion, rather than shock, and continued to do extraordinary work with her thanks to focusing on the human being in the moment.

'I don't give up and I won't give up'

While the one client who tried to walk out on me was unable to because of how prison works with locked doors, CIAO prefers a slightly more managed approach to stopping coaching. Effectively each person has six hours which we use as and when the coach and client wish to. This can edge up towards eight hours if sessions are a little longer, but that is the absolute limit to ensure we foster self-reliance not dependency. We stop sessions if it does not feel right for the client, without the client 'losing' a session. We can also pause and space sessions out, though the longer we take, the greater the risk of being unable to coach a client if they leave the prison.

Coaching is not for everyone, and we cannot prescribe who it does work for. Nor would we want to limit its application without good reason, particularly as CIAO has now shown through our work with male offenders in prison and in the community that its impact can be just as great there.

What clients need for coaching to work echoes the criteria outlined in Chapter 3. If these are missing then coaches are staring up a sheer cliff, rather than facing an uphill struggle. We could fix our own anchor points and climb up, but the energy to reward ratio is less likely to make it worth our while. Clients need a glimmer of possibility that things might change. They must want to be coached, or at least be curious about it, rather than being there because 'I was told I had to do it.' This includes a willingness to accept support and challenge, rather than sitting with crossed arms staring out of a window. Being able to think clearly without being affected by drugs is essential too. However, if a connection can be made without absolute clarity at first, then rapport with the coach can prompt the client to be motivated to be in the right place the next time. In an ideal world, they would also feel a level of personal connection with their coach.

Coaches can be reluctant to let go and realize or acknowledge when someone is not on form or, indeed, not ready for coaching. Instead we can desperately try to get them to be 'in the room'. This happened with Marie whom I met 11 times over the course of two months with just three solid sessions of an hour or so each near the start. On half of the occasions she turned up she was too distraught or distracted to be coached because: she was thinking she might have caught hepatitis from another woman's toothbrush; she had broken up with her girlfriend in Styal; she might be moved to another prison; and because another prisoner had died. Each time there was a reason. She was unaware we were meant to be meeting at all for the other times and there was no way for either of us to know how the message had not got through. Our processes and presence in the prison, including 'sorry to miss you' notes, would help avoid this situation now. I smiled to see in my client file that she had said: 'I don't give up and I won't give up.' This epitomized my approach too. However, sometimes giving up is the best thing to do. The prison had asked me to work urgently with Marie, as she seemed on the brink of moving forward or going down-hill. This may have fuelled my determination and clouded my judgement. It certainly should have rung alarm bells for me to ensure I checked in with someone else more regularly about our progress. Whether or not she was deliberately using me, it became clear now was not the right time for her to be coached, even if she benefited from our initial sessions. If I was not still acting as a coach then there was no point giving my attention to meet some other need in the client, nor a need in me to show coaching could 'work' for everybody.

Weighing up how ready a client is for coaching against our time spent waiting for them to be with us physically and mentally is a common chal-lenge. Another coach said: 'some clients are easier than others and some rapport is deeper than others. I also learnt to admit when coaching is not right and to have the courage to suggest it ends prematurely'. I might have felt I could do more if I worked in the prison and could see Marie regularly, etc., etc., but we do not and I could not. More importantly, the client has to take some responsibility, however chaotic life might be. So instead we met briefly to review all she had achieved and said goodbye.

Every client takes up a lot of head space, more so than professional ones because there is so much more background processing relating to the environment. I am not the only coach to notice this: 'It's fascinating. Each one is different and interesting. There's so much to think about, pre-pare and talk about.' Being in the right frame of mind for coaching and for the prison is essential. Coaching without your full faculties, whether in grief or exhaustion, is not a good idea.

While we make sure women are clear how to cancel sessions and are happy for them to do so, even if they simply do not feel they will do it justice, I got this very wrong the day after we buried one of our cats. The reason I went in regardless on that Saturday morning was to run a group session with coaches who had not worked with a room full of women, so I did not want to cancel it because of the many people involved. If it had just been me and one client I would definitely have stayed at home. The nuances of what others are saying and the impact my own words had were far harder to assess and react to in my grief. My struggling to remember the word 'articulate' was probably a clue. In spite of this the client I worked most with one-to-one in the group scored the session 3 out 10 for enjoyability and 8 for usefulness. She got what she wanted from the day and I was very surprised to read that she said the best thing was the 'strong forceful counsellor'. Two other clients fortunate enough to be coached by someone else gave her perfect 10s and their best things were: 'Learning that my head understands but getting my heart to as well' and 'That I wasn't pushed into anything I didn't want. My coach never put words in my mouth. She made me realize my values and reachable goals.' So my well-intentioned mistake did some good in the end and the comment that gave me the most hope was: 'That things can change.'

10   How did it go?

Coaches continue to underestimate what we can do, just as much as our clients. I am in awe of what clients and coaches have achieved. The coach who was unsure what difference we could possibly make in six hours later said: 'It's constantly surprising me in doing what it's doing. I really wasn't expecting this kind of change.' This chapter looks at that change through others' eyes and explores the statistics and independent research CIAO has gathered before looking at the impact on the coaches and how clients chose to 'pay it forward'.

CIAO has worked with well over 300 clients over its first four years. This is equivalent to about 8 per cent of the national female prisoner population. We have also coached men, in prison and out. We have sought to evidence the impact of our coaching from the start. Scores matter to our clients and our customers, as numbers help them see, as well as feel and know, the difference they have made to their lives. The following statistics took more effort to collect. I tried gathering them from coaches with an elegant IT solution but reverted to an old-fashioned, labour-intensive approach. I had forgotten it's best to be as human as possible and if there's one thing people know how to make a mess of, it's spreadsheets. Security and confidentiality affect who can input and analyse data as well, so the joy of pushing to collect the scores and playing with the monitoring and evaluation spreadsheets was mine and mine alone for the first two and a half years. It cheered me up no end when I was despairing that a client had gone off the radar before we did her final Star and a coach said: 'The fact that we get any data is amazing.'

The overall positive change on the Outcomes Star's objective scale was up 19 after coaching. This is two-thirds of the maximum possible improvement. The greatest shifts were in self-reliance and social capital – i.e. 'Motivation and taking responsibility' and 'Social networks and relationships'. Clients are not just after high scores, either. One kept her

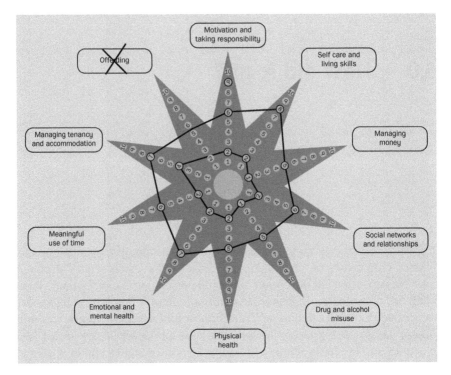

Figure 10.1 Lowest Outcomes Star scores (before and after coaching) in 2011
© Triangle Consulting Social Enterprise. See www.outcomesstar.org.uk

relationships at 7 because, even though she was very clear this area had improved significantly, she had raised her expectations of it accordingly.

When I analysed the lowest scores for 'Emotional and mental health' they were 2 before coaching and 7 afterwards (Figure 10.1 shows the lowest scores for every area on the Star). I initially doubted my spreadsheet and double-checked, but my formulae were right. This means that the worst position any one of our clients was in went up all the way from 2 to 7. The most dramatic improvement was from 2 to 9.5 (and that client not wanting to score herself a perfect 10 is telling in itself). These changes mean the difference between being stuck at the description: 'I don't like feeling like this but there is nothing anyone can do about it', to learning to make better choices and being able to agree: 'I mostly feel fine – I just need support now and then'. This huge shift turned out to be across the board, bar accommodation, perhaps because this generally needs a physical rather than mental movement. The increase in the lowest scores in all other areas was from an initial score of 1 or 2 (effectively not or only fleetingly considering change) up to a minimum of 5 (conscious desire for change). For someone who loves the meaning behind numbers that still gives me a thrill.

For most people though, whatever story the statistics tell, the clients themselves say so much more: 'I can deal with things on my own now, I am off anti-depressants. I've trained as a coach and done some coaching myself.'

The coaches want to know what happened next once clients are released as much as anyone. We do not know for most, but occasionally we bump into them and have feedback such as:

> She asked me to tell you that she's now got her daughter back. She went to court for the custody hearing and really stood up for her-self, just focused on the facts and not getting emotional, and now her daughter is back living with her and they are both really happy about it.

Or we heard from probation about a client who was doing really well months after she was released and was a 'completely different person' now, whereas she could not even make eye contact before. She had coped well with difficult family situations, was working and stood out as a supporter to others.

Outside views

As well as our own collection and analysis of quantities and quotes, we have been fortunate in obtaining formal independent external evalua-tion by people who gave their time without payment in the spirit of how CIAO operates. We began with the social accounts I wrote in 2012, which described the start and the impact of our coaching in Styal. A draft of these was tested by a qualified independent social accountant and auditor and by an impartial panel from criminal justice and health agencies, who both agreed it accurately reflected our work and impact.

Another independent view came from the Centre for Social Justice's paper on 'Meaningful Mentoring' in the criminal justice system. This described CIAO as 'ground-breaking', 'outstanding' and 'professional'. How-ever, I obviously failed to clarify the essential difference between coaching and mentoring because the report recommended that each new organiza-tion replacing probation 'sets up a professionally staffed women's mentor-ing unit which uses programmes based on models mentioned above', and ours was one of those two models.

Manchester Metropolitan University's independent evaluation of CIAO during 2013 then established that '94% of those interviewed reported that coaching had a positive impact on them, in making the best of their time in prison, in planning for release and living in the community'. This corrobo-rated our evidence by triangulating what clients and coaches said with the views of others inside and outside the prison. It also looked at our broader impact within the prison and community, as well as reductions in reoffending. I have used many of the quotes the researcher captured alongside mine in this book and he also said:

> Many of the women we were able to speak to presented coaching with an almost evangelistic fervour... 'It's the best thing the prison's ever done.' Virtually all spoke directly or indirectly of it boosting their confidence and self-worth, and of this in turn equipping them to better deal with problems in and/or out of prison.
>
> We were able to seek independent corroboration of what eleven clients told us... by speaking to people working in the prison and in probation (eighteen in all) about their perception of the women and if/how they had changed. In all but one case (where no change was perceived – the prisoner was always well-behaved) that corroboration was given. Staff believed coaching was contributing to the effectiveness of other initiatives and probation staff spoke of 'coaching as a very useful shortcut to readiness... it put women in a position to consider and work on issues through other interventions.' Another spoke of women who had been coached taking greater advantage of what was on offer within the prison and showing signs of positive planning for their remaining time inside and following release. [In a client's words:] 'I'm not being negative any more. I'm going to get as much out of here as possible.'
>
> [Over half interviewed] did consider that coaching had at least reinforced their resolve and ability to avoid further offending, and in some cases achieved more [and two] linked their offending to substance misuse which they clearly stated they had now put behind them, with the aid of coaching... Others spoke of how new skills or a new outlook or a new sense of self-worth would help them avoid the kind of situation which had given rise to their conviction. Many of these were not the conventional 'criminogenic needs' which criminologists tend to link to offending..., but the women were able to make the link... Even where such direct connections were not drawn, the increased control over their lives espoused by most of our interviewees is supported by research as raising the prospects of desistance: 'There is evidence that desisters have to "discover" agency (the ability to make choices and govern their own lives) in order to resist and overcome the criminogenic pressures that play upon them.'

We do not claim to be perfect though:

> coaching appeared to be generally well – or at least neutrally – regarded by those we spoke to in Styal, with just one exception... one person

employed within, but not by the prison…While he had come across women who raved about coaching, he could see no discernible impact on their behaviour…'

'You're always smiling, you lot! Why's that?'

This question about why we are always smiling, asked by a member of prison staff working on the gate, contrasts dramatically with a researcher elsewhere describing how just listening and absorbing vulnerable women's stories took its toll on her:

> No one warned me about going into a women's prison before. I came out and sat in my car and cried, feeling overwhelmed by the conversations I'd been having. It doesn't have that impact on me going into men's prisons.

I have never cried listening to a client in Styal and have been surprised how I could react without flinching or tears of sympathy to the most horrific stories. I have had tears in my eyes, but they do not get in the way of my coaching. Another coach did cry and her client said 'but you're supposed to make me cry'. The thing most likely to cause tears is the positive emotion when my clients make a breakthrough or read their final certificate with pride. Perhaps tears might have flowed had I not been coaching. Tales being mostly from the past helps, as a coach can help a client do all they can to change the present and the future.

Conversely, most of my clients inside have cried, whereas I cannot remember any professional clients doing so. We can both normalize and share those emotions as an act of humanity. Another coach said:

> The first couple of sessions she just cried and I thought 'Is there anything I can offer? I felt I was drowning with her. Then at the next session she said, 'You were absolutely right last time'…It sometimes feels as though we aren't doing anything but something works when one person gives their time and attention to another human being. You have to trust the process.

I have never worked with a client without her laughing either. With me and at me. If you take life completely seriously I do not see how it can possibly be worth living.

For us the positive impact on the coaches and what we have learnt about ourselves has been just as great as that on our clients:

It has been one of the most amazing things: a shift into this world knowing nothing and being quite frightened to having no qualms and no moments of anxiety, worry or fear for myself. It doesn't take up most of my time but it is the greatest thing in terms of its significance, importance and interest. People are impressed as well. It's such an interesting thing to tell people about. I learn what I'm getting from it when I tell others how much I've learnt and how much I know.

Other coaches said:

It's absolutely no different coaching anyone ... but in a different world ... It's worth all the hassle of the security and terror of the systems and processes. The fear of being publicly humiliated when you get it wrong. At last it's worth it. This is why I came. We get what we want as coaches *and* they get what they want as clients.

Coaching another human being: there's nothing different. We could be anywhere. It's another human being with particular struggles and challenges. I wanted to know that was true and it is. There are circumstantial things that are different but there are very similar basic human patterns, fears, hopes, needs and values that make them similar.

One coach was surprised by 'how much I enjoyed both clients' company and how easy it was to work together'.

Coaches have also been inspired by one another and by their clients:

This is just the best job I've ever had. I've never been in a group trying to do something where people have all been so positive. I always feel energized.

I coached a lifer and she was still optimistic despite having had her freedom taken for over a decade. She still had an inspiring attitude about what she'd do when she got out. She inspired me to change my approach to life and made me think: if I hadn't had the opportunities I've had, if I'd been in some of their circumstances, then where would I be now?

The coaches meet together and share the techniques that have helped our clients learn and move forward. We develop our skills with those who share our passion and understand the challenges. Our annual development weekends and wide variety of training tap into the many strengths and skills of our experienced and talented group as well as those of friends and contacts. We use facilitated 'action learning' too, where a group asks someone questions to prompt ideas and insight into the issue that individual wants help with. This uses the same technique as our coaching, so we can try questions out, learn and reflect safely. This helps us share experiences, work through personal and emotional issues and observe colleagues 'at work' in an authentic way, rather than role-playing.

Every coach can need practical and emotional back up, as well as the protection and security the prison provides. This is why our peer support pairs more and less experienced coaches. We use specific prompts relating to coaching in the prison to consider other perspectives and ideas on issues that may affect the prison, client or coach. This is essential as, while many coaches have their own coaching supervisor, working in the criminal justice system raises security issues we cannot discuss outside CIAO. Writing up their notes helps some process the learning and possible security and safeguarding issues as well. I have used other coaches as a sounding board to see if my plans are in the best interests of my client, rather than meeting any needs of my own, such as curiosity or for closure. We all have the numbers of a few coaches we can text to ask for emergency support at all times of day if needed. I've spoken with another coach on a mobile above the noise of an extractor fan while cooking an evening meal many a time.

As a result of this support and development as individuals and as a group, we were able to note self-esteem, personal growth and hope as outcomes for both clients and for the coaches themselves in the social accounts, along with quotes like: 'I'm more proud of what I've done in the last six months than what I've spent a lifetime doing as part of a career.'

'The realization that they can offer genuine help to other people'

From our first client onwards most of those we coach then want to make a positive contribution and help others in the community on a paid or voluntary basis, and this was part of our initial aims. On the simplest level a client said: 'Helping a friend made me a stronger person' while another:

> uses what she's learnt every day and is now keen to help others. She told me she is now training to be a Samaritans listener in prison; she is doing a counselling course so she can work with probation; and she has been asked to be a peer mentor.

Yet professionals say to me: 'volunteering never crossed my mind'. While that is not something to feel bad about, if you do not have the joy of giving some of your time for free in your life then you are missing out. As a coach said: 'Working with these clients has renewed my hope in humanity ... They both worked hard to do everything I asked of them and seemed to want to make a difference to themselves and to everyone around them.'

At least two of our clients became coaches themselves. This seems the ultimate accolade. Not least their wanting to share what they have benefited from but also, as our evaluation noted: 'the realization that they can offer genuine help to other people'. The other coach whose client did this said: 'It drew us closer together: she was the same as me, not someone who was inside for years.'

I bumped into a client who had trained as an alcohol recovery coach and realized we were now simply two professionals chatting and sharing ideas and techniques. She said she spent most her day giving advice as a mentor and then, when she was coaching:

> all of a sudden I've got to keep my mouth shut, so they can do it themselves. Not everyone has the same addiction, so I can't rely on what worked for me. But I can still help them by giving them confidence in themselves – and their ability to find their own solutions.

That conversation was one of my best moments with CIAO. I cannot imagine a better demonstration of the extraordinary power of coaching than someone who shared her deep pain with me, and then gave me permission to share the pain of her story with you in this book, becoming a valued coach herself.

That's why we're smiling.

11   Through the gate and beyond

Tales of what happened when clients were let out through the prison gate are scattered throughout this book and our coaching beyond bars is another book in itself. Through the gate is when it gets even harder as an ex-prisoner, as a coach or as an organization. However difficult you might have thought it was cracking the system from the inside, once you're outside the world becomes infinitely more complex. This is how it can hit women, how it was for CIAO as we grew and how it hit me.

It was like being in a twisted version of the Big Brother house when I saw an officer call a woman down from a dormitory and say: 'You're being released.' After a stunned pause she said: 'What? Today?' and was told: 'Yes, now, Pack up your things.' It seemed completely unexpected as she turned tearfully to her friends at the office door. She returned five minutes later with a clear plastic binbag she had thrown her things into while saying goodbye to her friends. I had asked my client, because of whom I was in the house in the first place, if she wanted to say goodbye too and she ran upstairs to do so in relieved delight.

Every time I am let back out, after just a few hours, I have a sense of freedom that I never feel leaving anywhere else. As another coach said: 'I walk away from here and I still think I'm the luckiest person on earth in comparison to the difficulties and circumstances women I've spoken to are in.' I never cease to be amazed at how little what I am told in the prison affects me. I can be with a client in an extreme emotional state without any feeling of helplessness because I have done all I can. The time I was grieving I was not the best coach for those clients, but still nothing affected me afterwards. Being fundamentally happy and fairly undamaged means clients' issues rarely trigger sensitivities. Getting on my bike and swooping down the steep slope Styal sits on is ideal for letting go of any trauma, heard or seen. The wind blows thoughts and feelings out of my head as I put distance between me and the prison. Driving back is never quite the same.

All the prisoners in Styal will be released at some point. Only a very small number held in other prisons with 'whole life tariffs' will never be let out. When someone can leave prison depends on their sentence, behaviour in prison and any time spent in prison waiting for their trial (on remand). Unknown and unclear dates mean clients are released without warning or do not come back from court, in a happy reversal of sudden imprisonment at the start. For security reasons the women themselves are given very little notice of moves. Whatever the case that means their coaching is over. We hope. Being released can be terrifying as well as joyful and coaching has helped with this: 'I'm not scared any more about the idea of getting out. I feel nervous but know what I want so can plan now'; 'She has set up plenty of support for when she gets out and this has been an important part of the coaching.'

Some women are met by family or friends, while others stand alone at the roadside clutching their few belongings in a binbag waiting for a lift or a bus. You get out and life hits you again: 'I bump into people. As soon as I come off the train. All the drug users hang out around the bus station drinking and stuff. There's no other way out.' Punishment rarely stops at the gate either. Society knows more about female offenders, as they are more unusual than male ones, so the media tell us more and the community can continue to judge and punish. Women recently released from prison are also 36 times more likely than the general population to kill themselves: 36 times more likely.

'Oh, you're back...'

This is not a simplistic tale of coaching as a miracle cure. I have seen four of my own 36 clients return to Styal and know Em went back into Holloway. It is not all bad though and when I was myself back inside coaching after a six-month absence I felt an odd mix of sadness and relief at seeing only four familiar faces among the women I bumped into. Fortunately I was able again to coach the four clients of mine who returned again. This was much more like working with clients in the community who are able to test and discuss all their new approaches, rather than only trying those ideas applicable inside. How did that go? What worked? What could you do differently? Where would you like to go now? I saw one of them, Louise, three times over three weeks before she was released one October. The next time I saw her, she was back in and we sat in the wing with festive decorations draped around us three days before Christmas. I was told by probation that 'she had been recalled [to prison, for breaching her licence] because her dad threw her out of the house mid-morning'. That was heartbreaking timing, yet she was able to reflect usefully on what she had learnt from her coaching and that experience. More importantly, I haven't seen her since.

For anyone whose life is bearable on the outside, being inside must be tough. Yet some prisoners view it as a sanctuary where they feel a sense of safety, support and community. One was greeted by another: 'Oh, you're back. That's great! How long are you in for? Three months? Fabulous!'

A crucial point though is that, whereas life outside may be too hard for some people, to get locked up you have to commit a crime, which requires a potential victim or victims. We know little about the impact on our clients' victims, but coaches' reflections like this give me hope:

> She was very scared of writing a letter to her victim because of the pain of coming to terms with and acknowledging what she had done. Whereas, at the start of coaching it was all about someone else being the main protagonist in the crime she'd committed. Much of this stemmed from a victim awareness course that she did, however, coaching gave her another avenue to explore and consolidate her thoughts and feelings. [She] wrote a letter to her victim acknowledging the impact of her offence and expressing regret... Watching a coachee move from not taking responsibility for her crime to acceptance and remorse was just amazing... She's come to terms with her responsibility for what she's done... She will teach [her baby son] to avoid fighting and that, whilst it may be hard to do something, it is important to do it anyway.

Growing up

No one in CIAO signed up for what we are doing now. I did not set out to create an organization, nor did I intend to start another charity – I thought the world had more than enough of those. At our very first meeting the extraordinary woman who would become the chair of our board shifted my thinking towards developing a social business providing coaching services that people would see the value of buying, rather than simply coaching for free. Initially we stayed unincorporated and did not seek funding for both simplicity and flexibility while we proved the worth of coaching inside and out. Instead, everyone gave their time, energy and skills without payment. This generosity equates to one person working full time for more than five years. Then on 20 March 2013 I registered CIAO as a company and we became a charity on 12 August 2013 with these objectives:

> The promotion of social inclusion among offenders and those who are or who have been at risk of offending, who are socially excluded from society, or parts of society as a result, by: providing coaching for such

persons; raising public awareness of the effectiveness of coaching for such persons; and providing support, training, development and consultancy to increase the availability of coaching for such persons.

In spite of taking this organic approach, or because of it, CIAO secured eight contracts outside the prison with four different customers. This developed our coaching with different client groups during 2013 and 2014: women in the community, women not on probation, men and families (including young people at risk of offending as well as offenders). Our only geographic restrictions are based on where people pay us to work outside Styal. None of our clients pay themselves. Three of those four customers have already renewed their contracts with us after seeing the successful impact of coaching on their clients.

I was aware from the start that it would be too messy for CIAO if I had another incident on my bike before we developed our resilience enough for me to be able to step away. I wanted to know the organization's future was secure with everything in place and all our knowledge in more than one head, so that no one was indispensable. This also meant ensuring we had funds to pay people to do what was currently being done for nothing. You need both money and love to make the world go round, so securing donations from people who believe in our work to pay for a part-time administrator was a great breakthrough. In my experience, changing the world is always underpinned by brilliant administrators who make things happen. Then, realizing we had brought in enough money of our own, through contracts, to be able to invest in other part-time support gave me my life back. The new roles enabled us to coach our clients as efficiently and effectively as possible, as well as helping CIAO grow. Four coordinators have also supported the coaches and engaged our clients. I continued to invest almost all my time and energies without salary for the first four years: many coaches continue to work without payment and some do not even claim expenses. I am pretty good at raising and earning money but hopeless at spending it. It took a lot of convincing for me to realize it is essential investment for CIAO to spend money to support me. This second breakthrough happened when I coincidentally met a prison philanthropist the day after I was too tired and in too much pain to do all the work I wanted to one weekend. Sometimes, like women we coach, I need to reach my limits and stare into a mirror to see sense.

We have shared our knowledge and philosophy nationally and internationally, both face to face and through articles, blogs and tweets. This has led others to set up services coaching veterans and young people, as well as offenders in general. I have talked about our work at the Criminology Institute at Cambridge, which is next door to the classics faculty where I studied among plaster casts of ancient statues, unaware I would later work in such a radically different field. Talking to the UK Association of Women Judges under the statue of the Greek goddess of wisdom at The Athenaeum made me smile too. What made me smile even more was when Clare Balding asked me if she could come into the prison and I saw women's faces as she spoke about her own failed attempt to break the law by shoplifting, before talking about regaining your self-belief and how to keep pushing yourself by asking 'What am I capable of today?'

All this growth and sharing happened while even well–established charities were chasing their tails keeping up with developments across the criminal justice system. That CIAO came of age during this very hard time makes me even more proud of the work of our coaches and the faith of all our funders and supporters.

The successes, whether for individual clients or the service as a whole, have remarkably little to do with me. I just started it off. That does not simply make me a catalyst though: a catalyst remains unchanged at the end of the reaction and I learnt more in my few years in Styal than in the previous decade. I would love to coach some clients again with all I have now learnt about me, them and coaching. But that misses the point of life. We are all doing all we can to the best of our ability in each moment. There is no need to relive and redo what we have done. Otherwise we would be caught in that hellish groundhog day Tess was so glad to escape from.

The gently boiled frog

The person whose growth I have been most stunned by is me. I have never been told I am very patient before and used to struggle with being part of organizations, though I loved working with them. This meant that setting up a company and then a charity was something of a strategic error, to say nothing of becoming managing director. At one point I heard myself say: 'I'm not sure there's enough for a full-time role... Oh... On the other hand I do work 70–80 hours a week...'

This has been the hardest year of my working life. In creating an organization to increase the sum total of human happiness I made myself miserable. I was doing the best I could and stretching myself to my limits, but that did not feel good enough. I wanted to resign but had no job or office to walk away from. I had given up my own freedom and built my own prison.

I was like the gently boiled frog, gradually losing my self-awareness. I thought I should have known how close I was to cracking, but I was on the inside. I really had to remind myself of all I had managed over the years, rather than thinking I might be unable to cope. I was so exhausted and overwhelmed with everything on my to do list that I lacked the energy to be logical and lay things out clearly for myself and others. Without a sharp mind I could not be efficient and my body stole two months from my brain over the course of the last year. I even postponed an operation to resolve this, as I did not want to risk what could be a real deadline before I had done enough for others to carry on without me.

Then the frog had the revelation that it deserved to be happy, not miserable. Three years after we began coaching I cried when I thought that if I had known CIAO was going to hurt me this much I was not sure I would have started it. I love people who challenge me. Eventually. My brain works overtime about what is going on mentally and emotionally while it is happening, but I love the final resolution and better outcome. However, this went too far for me when some could not sense or were unable to respond positively to the pressure I was under. Fortunately, we cannot see into the future and, as soon as I was no longer in physical pain, I knew I would not change what I had been through for anything. Ironically what saved me from the bruising spiral, other than the ceaseless support of extraordinary people in CIAO, was having the energy to stop. So that was what I did, however briefly, as soon as I possibly could. I was light years from my comfort zone for months and needed a break from that tension. Apparently I never stopped laughing though. That would have been a deeply worrying sign.

Fortunately, I am good at falling but just as good at getting back up again: two useful skills in life. Helping people to change and even find a reason to keep on living is very powerful motivation, but I am still amazed I have made it this far.

Getting stuck in

When stuck inside, at the start, it was only when I stood staring at the locked gate that the reality of prison struck me. Fortunately, all it took to secure my release was a few moments of feeling sheepish until someone could confirm who I was. For most of our clients, getting out and staying out is a lot tougher. It is a gift to be aware of your freedom. Even now I never walk out through that prison gate without learning, seeing or hearing something that makes me reconsider or value my life even more.

The freedom of our minds is even more of a gift. CIAO has enabled me to realize that taking an approach that is all about self-determination, that is so valued and potent in industry, can still transform lives when it is taken into an environment that is perhaps the least self-determining you can get. If coaching can work there, it can work anywhere.

We have also seen how our prisons are full of potential that can be unlocked through the power of questions alone. Working out who we are and what we really want is something almost all of us struggle with at some point. To say nothing of the occasional or, for some, constant struggle of our lives as a whole.

The reason I do what I do is because I don't know what I would have done were I some of those clients I've had the pleasure of working with inside. Even if you think you have been in someone else's situation, you have not lived their entire life. Similarly, if you think someone else has less potential to change and grow than you, then you hold us all back.

Coaching can bring two human beings together with the respect and belief of each magnifying that of the other. Humanity helps clients and coaches transform their lives in ways they would never previously have imagined. For, as Alex showed after her desperate search for it, no one is beyond hope, even behind bars.

How can you make a difference?

If, after reading this book, you would like to join the many people making a positive impact behind bars, then here are some ways you might coach, write to, visit or work to support offenders and their families in other ways. You can also follow the CIAO website for more news and stories of our coaching on both sides of the gate.

Coaching Inside and Out (CIAO)

CIAO would love to hear from experienced coaches who would like to join us or from organizations who would like to work with us. Check the website to see where we are working now. We may also know of other services near you.

www.coachinginsideandout.org.uk

Clinks

Clinks is a national charity that supports voluntary and community organizations working with offenders. Search their Directory of Offender Services for other ways you might help. You can also keep informed by signing up for their weekly national e-newsletter 'Light Lunch'.

www.clinks.org

Independent Monitoring Boards

Every prison has an Independent Monitoring Board (IMB). This is a group of ordinary, unpaid members of the public who have unrestricted access to monitor day-to-day life and ensure standards of care and decency. Members can talk to any prisoner they wish.

www.justice.gov.uk/about/imb

New Bridge

Volunteers offer letters and visits to prisoners who request them, particularly to those who have no one else who supports them in this way. No qualifications or previous training are required and this was where I started out.

www.newbridgefoundation.org.uk

Resilience
A practical guide for coaches

Carole Pemberton

ISBN: 978-0-335-26374-5 (Paperback)
eBook: 978-0-335-26375-2
2015

Resilience: A Guide for Coaches is based on the author's experience as an expert executive and career coach. Inspired by her own research with individuals who have lost their resilience; it provides key insights from psychology, case study evidence and tools for coaches to work with on resilience issues.

Practicing or training coaches can gain:

- An understanding of what resilience is, and what separates it from burnout and trauma
- A range of approaches that they can use in working with resilience issues
- A better understanding of the their own resilience

OPEN UNIVERSITY PRESS
McGraw - Hill Education

www.openup.co.uk